JOSEPH FARRELL

DARIO FO AND FRANCA RAME:

PASSION UNSPENT

Ledizioni

© 2015 Ledizioni LediPublishing
Via Alamanni, 11 – 20141 Milano – Italy
www.ledizioni.it
info@ledizioni.it

Joseph Farrell, *DARIO FO AND FRANCA RAME: PASSION UNSPENT*

Images on the appendix are taken from "Archivio di Franca Rame Dario Fo".
Cover: graphic design by Pietro Virtuani, from Ledizioni Srl

First edition: May 2015

Print ISBN   9788867053230
Ebook ISBN   9788867053247

Catalogue and reprints information: www.ledizioni.it

CONTENTS

DARIO FO AND FRANCA RAME:
PASSION UNSPENT

To Francis, Catriona, Lucy and Anna

INTRODUCTION

It is now a cliché to repeat that even if no longer in his salad days, Dario Fo, born on 24 March 1926, remains the most performed playwright of modern times, while it is equally clichéd to repeat that the award of a Nobel Prize can, however paradoxical it may seem, represent a crisis in the life of a creative writer. How can the Nobel laureate live up to the standards a world-wide community now expects of him or her? This short work attempts to consider how Dario, awarded the Nobel for Literature in 1997, has responded to that challenge and has taken advantage of the higher public profile the award brought with it to expand the range of public issues for which he campaigns, as well as continuing his work as playwright and performer. In addition, while involving himself in the politics of Milan and Italy, he has devoted more time and energy than previously to painting, and has authored many books of art criticism and of social, political and cultural history.

This level of output is impressive in itself, but does create problems for the conscientious critic or biographer, and indeed it has become clear in the course of writing these chapters on Dario's later life that even if modern publishers afforded authors the Victorian luxury of the three-volume work, it would still be impossible to write a satisfactory biography of Fo, one half of one of the most astonishing couples in the history of Italian and European theatre. Dario and Franca have simply done too much, written too much, spoken too much, given too many interviews, made too many television programmes, supervised too many workshops, been involved in too many controversies, appeared too often on stage, performed in too many countries, have had too many plays translated into too many languages, and have travelled too much for any one book to provide a complete record of their lives and achievements. Not even Dario Fo can have read all that has been written by Dario Fo, let alone about Dario Fo. Too much has been written about them in too many languages and their impact has been felt in too many countries for any one biographer to be able to do justice to all their achievements, even if the aim were to deal only with their theatrical work. Franca has certainly facilitated the biographer's task, since she has shown herself to be an astonishing archivist who has collected everything written about them in every language of every country they have visited since they first worked together. The mass of material is impressive, and overwhelming. There are articles on their work not only in European languages such as English, French and Catalan but also in Asian languages like Chinese, Japanese and Farsi. Who could digest them all?

They have been chroniclers of, and participants in, many of the great events which have shaped modern Italy, which means they have been in equal measure supported and opposed, loved and hated, admired and vilified, revered and persecuted. The fact that in the course of their lives they were assaulted in Argentina, that the American government twice found it necessary to refuse them visas, that the Vatican attacked them, that Soviet authorities refused to license their plays for performance, that bombs have been placed near their homes and theatres, that Franca was kidnapped and raped with the connivance of the police forces and that they have faced prosecution on many occasions in Italy is proof, however desperate the expression of that proof, of their national and international status as spokespersons for causes unpopular with those who wield power.

This book examines a short time frame, approximately from the award of the Nobel Prize to Dario until the present day as Dario approaches his ninetieth birthday, but even within those limits what is offered here can be regarded as a miniature of the sort which was popular in the England of Shakespeare. Nicholas Hilliard, an artist in that tradition, attempted to reproduce the main features of the person portrayed, but was aware of what had to be omitted. I have attempted to look not only at the theatre of Dario and Franca, but also at their political campaigning and at the social and the individual causes they championed, as well as at Dario's painting and his recent work of criticism of the great Italian artists. At an age when most would relax into the ease of retirement, they continued writing articles and participating in movements for change in many fields. Examples include their work for reform of the prison system, for the abolition of the death penalty in countries where it is still legal and for the rethinking of official policies on drugs and on pollution. They both also became spokespersons against bio-engineering and cloning, and have taken up issues associated with ecology and green politics. Finally both came into the arena of active politics, Franca as a senator and Dario as candidate for mayor of Milan and then as active supporter of the 5 Star Movement founded by the ex-comedian Beppe Grillo. After the death of Franca, Dario has continued on his own.

A separate study could be made of the reputation of Dario Fo and Franca Rame in different countries in the world. I once turned up at their house in Milan to discover Dario in conversation, of a sort, with three actors from Sri Lanka. None of the three Sri Lankans spoke Italian, but one of them was making efforts to express himself in English, which was somewhat futile, since Dario has no knowledge of the language. The four were communicating by random and ill-focused gestures and by looking vacantly at production photographs of Dario in various roles. The visitors listened intently and uncomprehendingly as he expatiated on the history of Italian theatre and the dilemmas of Italian politics, and he in his turn listened with an expression which suggested that the spirit was willing but the ear inadequate as they told him how much he was honoured in their country. He got the idea that they admired Accidental Death of an Anarchist and thought they might be seeking permission to stage Can't Pay! Won't Pay!, but had not understood that they were saying that these two plays had been already produced and that the depiction of a dissident mysteriously killed in police custody, or the description of people driven by desperation to take the law into their own hands, had struck a cord with them.

There is a further challenge. Franca has complained on several occasions of being written out of the script, or of being reduced to the status of pedestal under the monument which is Dario. The two have mainly, but not invariably, seen eye to eye on theatre and politics and there have been at times difficulties in personal relations, including one celebrated occasion in 1987 when Franca announced on national television that she had left Dario, but theirs has been a deep, lasting and fruitful collaboration. Unpicking the contribution of the one or the other is a difficult and perhaps pointless task. The best that can be done is to keep the dual nature of their work in view.

These chapters can be viewed as an addendum to my earlier biography - *Dario Fo and Franca Rame: Harlequins of the Revolution* (London, Methuen, 2001), which ends approximately with the award of the Nobel Prize. An Italian translation was published as *Dario e Franca: la biografia della coppia Fo/Rame attraverso la storia italiana* (Milan, Ledizioni, 2014), and I took advantage of the publication of that edition to revise the original work and to update it with some new chapters which took the story up to the death of Franca Rame in May 2013. These new chapters had not previously been made available in English, and make up the bulk of the present work. However, I have revised the work further to make intelligible to English-language readers matters which would not have required explanation to an Italian. Dario has not stopped writing, painting, performing, campaigning, lecturing and appearing on TV shows, so this short book has been again updated.

There are many people to whom I am indebted. My principal debt is to Franca Rame for her patience and willingness to spend time with me answering questions. I mourn her passing and regret that she will not see the result. I am grateful to Dario Fo for many enjoyable, stimulating and informative conversations. I would also like to express gratitude to Walter Valeri, Ron Jenkins, Piero Sciotto, Paolo Puppa, Vittorio Franceschi, Tony Mitchell, Antonio Scuderi, Tom Baldwin and Ed Emery. Chiara Porro, one of Dario's personal assistants, showed great kindness in answering questions and helping me find documents. I owe a debt too to some who are no longer with us, Emilio Tadini, Flavia Tolnay, Bianca Fo Garambois, Chris Cairns and Nanni Ricordi, and others who preferred not to be named. I am extremely grateful to the publishers Nicola and Lorenzo Cavalli for their many kindnesses. It was Nicola who suggested that these chapters should be made available in English. I cannot quantify my debt to my wife, Maureen.

Chapter I

DARIO AND FRANCA: HIGHLIGHTS OF ONE CAREER

In the official citation explaining the decision to award the 1997 Nobel Prize for Literature to Dario Fo, the Swedish Royal Academy stated that he had 'emulated the jesters of the Middle Ages in scourging authority and upholding the dignity of the downtrodden.' It went on to add that 'with a blend of laughter and gravity, he opens our eyes to abuses and injustices in society ... Fo is an extremely serious satirist.' It is an acute judgment. Fo is an altogether more complex figure than has been appreciated by either admirers or critics who are familiar only with his big political farces. His finest theatre is set in an uncertain area between the Wasteland and Wonderland, a vantage point which permits him to observe the political and social detritus of modern society and to scourge the holders of power by employing satirical wit, fantasy, inventiveness and even nonsense of a sort which would not have been out of place in Jonathan Swift or Lewis Carroll.

While he is a playwright many of whose scripts have been inspired by the headlines of the day, as is the case with such overtly polemical works as *Morte accidentale di un anarchico*, (1970, Accidental Death of an Anarchist), or *Non si paga? Non si paga!* (1974, Can't Pay? Won't Pay!), and others whose themes have been suggested by the concerns of his audience, for instance the work on the drugs problem, *La marijuana della mamma è la più bella*, (Mum's Marijuana is the Best, 1976), his roots are deep in the theatrical traditions of Italy. He has chosen at different times to identify himself with the quintessentially medieval figure of the 'jester', (probably the best translation of the Italian term *giullare)*, or with the Harlequin of *commedia dell'arte*, even when writing on contemporary issues. In 1968, that year of demonstrations, occupations and protests against war and against all that went under the name 'bourgeois' or 'capitalist,' he broke with the conventional, commercial theatre where he had seen so much success with critics and audiences, to set up his own cooperative troupe to play in an 'alternative' circuit of venues. On that occasion, he made the announcement whose full import was missed at the time, that he was tired of being the *giullare* of the moneyed classes and would henceforth be the *giullare* of the proletariat. At precisely the moment when he decided that his theatre would challenge the society of his own time, he turned to the past to find his model.

The break itself was inevitable in the climate of the times and in view of the dissatisfaction he had been experiencing with his own success in commercial theatre. Others before him, including Henrik Ibsen and George Bernard Shaw, had noted to their exasperation that the targets of their satirical jibes reacted with amused tolerance, or even indifference, since the barbs and jibes were, they believed, aimed at their neighbours, not at them. Dario employed the colourful expression that he had been consumed as a refreshing alka seltzer by those who upheld the very system he was out to undermine. In future, as *giullare* of the proletariat he would fight for better tomorrows by taking on the guise of a theatrical figure from the past. It cannot be stated too strongly that Fo is a traditionalist as well as iconoclast, and an iconoclast in search of a tradition to uphold as much as to overturn. He is a revolutionary in politics but a conservative in theatre. He has never had any truck with the *avant-garde* or with experimental theatre, a style of performance particularly strong in Italy.

He is also an actor-author, a figure more central to the Italian tradition of theatre than his equivalent in other countries, a figure who can be taken as the "representative man" of Italian theatre in the sense that term was used by Ralph Waldo Emerson in his collection of biographical essays of that title. Dario's preferred genre is farce, but this is neither the ideas-free knockabout of the boulevardiers, nor the metaphysical angst of the post-war Absurdist writers but what can be defined as didactic farce, a wholly new style of farce with a purpose. Other paradoxes are also adumbrated in the citation by the 'Immortals' of Stockholm's Academy. He may be a farceur, but as a satirist he is a deeply serious writer, whose laughter expresses not levity but anger and who cares about the abuses of society and the plight of those who are euphemistically described as the underprivileged.

The award of the Nobel prize was highly controversial in Italy not only among political opponents but also with critics, who may have admired him as an actor but who regarded his writing with lofty disdain. Indeed, the one group which has consistently declined to recognize the achievements of Dario and Franca is the Italian intelligentsia, even those who are left-leaning. However odd it may be in a country where under the inspiration of Antonio Gramsci intellectuals have been engaged on a search for the 'national-popular' tradition, they failed to recognise that quality in Fo, perhaps because no one has developed the critical tools for judging exponents of popular culture. There is not in Fo any of the 'ambiguity' so much admired in the major playwrights of the western tradition. In the Italian tradition, he is not a descendant of, for example, Luigi Pirandello, for whom he has scant respect and whom he regards as tedious and elitist. His antecedents are to be found in the by-ways of theatre history, specifically in the traditions of popular theatre, where 'popular' has the sense conferred on it by Gramsci, of belonging to the people as distinct from the ruling orders. Fo admires above all Ruzante, an actor-author active of the late Renaissance, and Molière, as well as obscure Harlequins, clowns and entertainers. His taste for farce was born of his own abilities and instincts, reinforced by the belief that it was pre-eminently the popular form of theatre.

Fo did not, in other words, spring to life in 1968, even if his best known plays date from that period. There is a recognised narrative to his intellectual and artistic development, some aspects of which he has sanctioned in interviews and in his whimsical autobiographical work *Il paese dei mezarat: I miei primi sette anni (e qualcuno in più*, 2002), (My First Seven Years). In this version, repeated in his Nobel lecture, he was introduced to popular culture and to the art of story-telling by the *fabulatori* (story-tellers) in the village of Valtravaglia on Lake Maggiore where he grew up. These men were not professional performers but fishermen or glass-blowers who told their tales as they mended nets or manufactured glass works. Walter Benjamin wrote that stories were customarily invented and recounted in the work-place by men and women whose aim was to keep at bay the boredom of repetitive labour, and so it was in the glass-works and the harbour by the lake. Children gathered to listen to tales which blended fantasy and satire and enshrined a vision of the world as seen by ordinary people, the underclass. In Stockholm, Dario retold the tale he had heard as a boy concerning the villagers of Caldè, another village on the lake. They were warned that their houses were subject to subsidence and were slipping under the water, but were too pig-headed to heed such advice, or too stupid to notice. As the village vanished under water, they continued living their day to day lives and going about their banal business, incapable of reacting to the fact that the community was totally submerged.

There is a continuity of technique and value between the angry, inventive whimsy of such stories and Dario's later monologues, such as *Johan Padan ala descoverta delle Americhe* (1991, Johan Padan in Quest of the Americas). Fo the dramatist is, among other things, a teller of tales. It was with radio monologues that he started his career as performer in the 1950s. The pieces he did then and in his first appearances on stage portrayed an upside-down world, where, for instance, Goliath is a jolly if inept giant and David an obnoxious little sycophant out to curry favour with his superiors. Fo had no official training as an actor, but moved from these monologues to apprentice work in Variety in Milan, where he met Franca Rame, whom he married in 1954. The Rame family were a troupe of travelling players who could trace their origins back to the nineteenth or possibly the eighteenth century, and who were in a wider sense heirs of *commedia dell'arte*. They produced drama based on improvisation in the towns and villages in Lombardy to which the family-company toured. Unlike Dario, Franca had theatre in her veins. Together the two set up their own company and in the late 1950s they staged two series of one-act farces, *Ladri, manichini e donne nude* (Thieves, Mannequins and Naked Women) and *Comica Finale* (End Piece), all written by Dario, although the second series was inspired by *canovacci* (outline scripts) used over the years by the Rame family, as they had been by Italian players since the heyday of *commedia dell'arte*. As at other points in his career, innovation and precedent go hand in hand. Some critics at the time viewed Fo as the Italian Ionesco or Beckett, but the antecedents, aims, ideal audience and traditions in which they operated were profoundly different.

Success led to an invitation to perform in the major theatres of the Italian cities, and ushered in a period from 1959 – 68 known as Fo's "bourgeois period." In those years, Dario wrote a comedy a year, often with music and song, performed first in the Odeon in Milan and then toured all over Italy. The term "bourgeois" is not a happy description, for while the venues were those which attracted a middle class audience, the plays themselves were works of biting satire on corruption and malpractice in business, in the church and in politics in those days when Italy was ruled by a series of short-lived, Christian Democrat governments. Censorship was still in force, and scripts had to be submitted for advance approval.

They were routinely returned from the censor's office rendered almost unperformable and unintelligible by the number of deleted lines. Little men in the stalls with torches scanning scripts must have made attendance at a play unpleasant for regular theatre-goers, but it must have been an equally frustrating experience for the officials themselves as they tried to reconcile the pages in their hands with the dialogue spoken on stage. A Fo play is always a work in progress, and so not easy to restrain. Franca took on herself the task of recording all the changes made as the run proceeded to produce a final version for publication.

All the plays in this period give a jaundiced view of those in power. The 1960 play, *Aveva due pistole e occhi bianchi e neri* (He had Two Pistols and Black and White Eyes) is set in a psychiatric hospital which resembles a monastery, thereby uniting satire of church and state, or more precisely poking fun at a state run by clerical forces and a church-dominated party. Dario took the two central roles of a priest who had lost his memory and a bandit on the run. His character is supposedly recognised by Luisa, played by Franca Rame, as her ex-lover, and she takes up with him again. Implausible coincidences multiply, but the satire struck home. The religious institution-asylum provided the background for *Settimo; ruba un po' meno*, (1974, Seventh Commandment: Steal a Little Less) where Franca, taking the main part for the first time, played the part of a gravedigger who forms a relationship with an accountant whose odd ways include sleeping in a coffin. Together they uncover evidence of widespread sleaze, but he is silenced by having his brain drilled and a curious rotating fan inserted in his skull. A farce it may be, but the vision behind it is bitter and violent.

Dario and Franca became increasingly uncomfortable with the compromise of entertaining the section of society he believed he was denouncing in his satire. In 1968, they announced they were leaving the commercial or bourgeois theatre circuit. Their intention was to establish a new kind of company, which would take theatre to places where drama had not been normally performed and to play for people who were not theatre-goers. Yet again this decision represented a return to roots, this time to the style of touring theatre Franca and her family had performed. The first company, *Nuova Scena*, was structured as a co-operative, but unlike many other similar troupes set up at that time, the theatrical means mattered as much as the ideological content. The company was close to the Communist party and played in its cultural and recreational centres, ARCI. The first work was a grand pageant, *Grande Pantomima, con bandiere e pupazzi piccoli e medi*, (1969, Grand Pantomime with Banners and

Large and Medium Puppets). The performers wore masks in the style of *commedia dell'arte*, and the set was dominated by a gigantic, grotesque puppet from whose womb emerged figures representing the Bourgeoisie, the Military and Capital.

His colleagues and comrades assumed that Dario would continue producing agit-prop pieces preaching revolution and exposing contemporary injustices, and were disconcerted or even outraged when he announced at a meeting of the troupe that his next work would be *Mistero buffo*, a series of one-man sketches based on medieval material which he had gathered from archives and libraries all over Europe. His belief was that it was vital to keep a popular tradition alive and that it was valuable to show the continuity between injustices suffered by peasants in the Middle Ages and those experienced now, a continuity he made clear in improvised introductions to the individual routines. He was convinced that medieval religious pageantry and ceremonial gave voice both to the people's entertainment and protest. The focus of medieval life was the church and on feast days, the people expressed both their joy and their anger. The connection in the English words holy-day and holi-day expresses the idea more clearly than the Italian equivalents. Popular culture, to which he was dedicated, had wider connotations than up to the minute political theatre.

Some episodes in *Mistero buffo* consist of complete medieval sketches Dario had uncovered in his researches but in others the original material was often no more than a few lines which he reworked, reinvented and enlarged. This show, added to over the years, has proved to be Fo's most enduring work. It has allowed him to display his talents as actor as well author, and to give body to his core cultural–political beliefs. The most successful pieces included *The Raising of Lazarus*, featuring the wide boys who sold their wares to the crowd gathered to witness the promised miracle. Christ is a figure who appears in the distance, like a film star at a premiere. *The Marriage Feast at Cana* is seen from the perspective of a drunk, while the *Birth of the Jester* can be regarded as a manifesto play. The central figure is a peasant whose lands are appropriated and family slaughtered by the local lord, but when he himself is on the point of suicide, he is approached by an enigmatic figure, who turns out to be Christ himself, who kisses him on the mouth to give him the gift of poetry and the ability to become a *giullare*, that is a spokesman who can give voice to the wrongs endured by ordinary people. The most controversial and successful piece was a savage satire on Pope Boniface VIII, a contemporary of Dante whom the author of the Divine Comedy detested and placed in hell. In his introduction, Dario made comic but not bitter reference to the contemporary pope, John Paul II. His satire was directed at the Church as institution and at the distance between its current stance and the preaching of Christ. Dario never attacks Christian doctrine as such. Boniface is a cruel, arrogant pontiff, who delights in pomp and circumstance but who as he parades round Rome suffers the indignity of being kicked in the backside by Christ.

Tensions developed inside *Nuova Scena* in part driven by ideological disputes and in part by personal factors. Perhaps the gulf between Fo's drive to express his innate abilities and his wish as an activist to commit to cooperative performance was unbridgeable. The troupe split up in some acrimony and Fo and Rame established in 1970 a new company, *La Comune*, a more managerially operated outfit which maintained some semblance of cooperative functioning. This group was more openly critical of the Communist party, which it viewed as having betrayed its revolutionary Marxist origins. It established a permanent home in a converted workshop in Milan, but was also committed to touring. The first work was *Accidental Death of an Anarchist*, premiered in December 1970. Together with *Mistero buffo*, this has been his most successful and frequently staged work, and shows the other side of Fo's creativity. The basic theme is more appropriate for tragedy than farce. In December 1969, a bomb laid by terrorists went off in a Milan bank killing sixteen people. The intricacies of the case and the consequences of the mendacity of the police and politicians have occupied the energies and attention of Dario and Franca all their lives, as is outlined in a later chapter. Briefly, in the immediate aftermath of the outrage, an innocent man, the anarchist Pino Pinelli, was arrested by the police, taken into custody in a police station from which he never emerged alive. Fo's play was conceived as an act of 'counter-information' to refute the official line that anarchists were responsible for the explosion and that Pinelli had committed suicide. It also advanced the theory, subsequently shown to be true, that the bombing was the work of neo-fascist elements operating in cahoots with the police and elements in the ministries.

Luigi Calabresi, the Inspector in the play, brought an action for libel against Pio Baldelli, the editor of *Lotta Continua*, a left-wing journal which had accused him of responsibility for Pinelli's death. The trial and the initial run of the play took place at the same time, and the script of the play was altered night by night to incorporate material produced at the trial, which ended when Calabresi was himself assassinated. The ramifications of this tragic case would return to the headlines in the 1980s, and would drag on well into the new millennium. In *Accidental Death*, Dario played the part of a madman with a genius for disguise, who is arrested by the very police force which had arrested Pinelli, who is never named in the play. An enquiry into the anarchist's death had been ordered, so the quick witted madman-impersonator takes on the role of the investigating magistrate, calls the officers to appear before him and combs over the various theories advanced to explain Pinelli's death. The work uses the rhythms and techniques of farce and has, to the surprise of many, enjoyed great success all over the world even with audiences who had no knowledge of the original case. The events recounted are wrapped in a flexible theatrical structure which has universal appeal, but directors elsewhere have struggled with the problem of combining political commitment with uproarious knockabout more commonly associated with Feydeau and boulevard farce.

By 1973, *La Comune* too was riven by internal dissent and broke apart. In a colourful expression used at the time, the company had become like a penny-farthing bicycle, where it was difficult for the large and the small wheel to move at the same pace. This was a catastrophic year in the life of the couple, who were by now accustomed to receiving death threats and menaces. Bombs were placed near theatres where they were to perform, and managers of booked venues were intimidated. In March, Franca was subjected to acts of the most brutal savagery when she was kidnapped, driven around Milan in a truck, tortured and repeatedly raped. No one doubted at the time that this atrocity was the work of right-wing thugs, but years later in 1998 it was established in a meticulously researched report by the magistrate Guido Salvini that the attack was done with the knowledge and indeed connivance of the *carabinieri*. President Oscar Luigi Scalfaro issued an official apology on behalf of the state. At the time the crime was committed, while it was known that Franca had been assaulted and abused, she did not make public the fact that she had been raped. Later she wrote a monologue entitled starkly *The Rape*, but did not initially perform it herself. Years passed before, in a gesture of support for moves to have the law on rape in Italy reformed, she admitted that the piece was based on her own experiences. Only then did she play the part herself. In November the same year, Dario and Franca were in Sassari to perform a play, *La Guerra del popolo in Cile* (The People's War in Chile), a denunciation of the American-backed coup d'état in Santiago which overthrew the Marxist President, Salvador Allende. The local *carabinieri* insisted on seeing the script, but Dario refused saying they had no rights in the matter. He was then arrested and spent the night in prison. Franca led a campaign to have him released and drew support from all sections of Italian society, excepting Pier Paolo Pasolini who chose that moment to define Fo as 'a plague for Italian theatre.'

The commitment of Dario and Franca to radical causes was unabated, but took new forms. With others they set up a reformed company with a more conventional managerial structure, and took over the art nouveau Palazzina Liberty, once a flourishing market building but now deserted and abandoned in the middle of a park in Milan. This was to be their home over the coming years, but it was also to be at the centre of a series of legal battles as the City Council, which had originally offered them the building but then rescinded the agreement, tried to have them evicted. *Can't Pay? Don't Pay!* was performed here in 1974. In accordance with a practice they had developed, the play was discussed with trade union and other groups in advance of staging. The script reflected the fact that inflation was a growing problem for people who saw their purchasing power diminish and who took matters into their own hands by "liberating" from supermarkets the goods and products they required, paying a price they themselves decided appropriate.

The main focus in those years was the changing role of women in society, a topic made central to left-wing agendas by the Women's Movement which was stronger in Italy than in most other European countries, and which had the full support of Franca Rame. Franca's role in the authorship of the plays performed and published by the couple over their career, and not only in this period, has been much debated, and will be discussed in a later chapter, but by her own account at this stage she pestered Dario to write something which reflected the dissatisfaction of contemporary women and their demands for change. He was, in other words, the main author. Her input was not limited to the performance, since she criticised and made suggestions, but this was well established practice with the couple. It is not clear that there was any change in this practice at this point. The best known result of their collaborative work of this period was a series of monologues published under various titles, *Parliamo di donne* (Let's Talk about Women), or *Parti femminili* (Female Parts)

Franca always declined to apply to herself the terms "feminist" and dismissed the overtly feminist theatre she had seen or had been sent to her for performance as heavy, whingeing, humourless and tedious, while she aimed at producing drama which was colourful, ironic, satirical and made serious points through the medium of comedy. Her monologues covered a wide range of topics and brought to life many individual courageous, forgotten women, such as the anti-Fascist Mamma Togni or the distraught mother of the mafia victim, Michele lu Lanzone. She used one monologue to protest against the treatment in custody of the German terrorist, Ulrike Meinhof, but also performed an idiosyncratic revision of the myth of Medea, and on another occasion overturned the story of Alice to produce *Alice in the Land Without Wonders*, which ended in a long scatological ramble. Her most successful pieces focused on concrete, day-to-day problems facing modern women. *Una donna sola* (A Woman Alone) features a woman in conversation with an unseen neighbour but coping at home with an intrusive, abusive, invalid brother-in-law and with obscene phone calls, while *Il risveglio* (The Alarm Clock) is a hilarious, high-octane piece on the morning routine of a working woman who dashes about the house getting herself and her baby ready to go out, mixing up what is needed to powder the baby's bottom and what is needed for breakfast, losing things, including the baby, in her haste, only to remember at the last moment that it is Saturday and that there is no work that day.

Franca took part in the campaigns for the legalisation of divorce and abortion and for the reform of rape laws, as well as other issues affecting women. Dario was equally active on many fronts. In 1987, he published *Manuale minimo dell'attore* (Tricks of the Trade), the recording of various workshops and lectures, a book which contains the most complete account of his poetics and is the nearest he came to producing a manifesto. He has never published a systematic account of his views on acting and playwriting, so his general ideas have to be deduced from his many occasional writings and interviews. *Totò, manuale dell'attor comico* (1991, Totò, Manual of the Comic Actor), his admiring account of the homonymous Neapolitan comic actor, is also of great value. These two works express Fo's views on the popular tradition, and his preference to have his political theatre viewed not as a deviation from, but as an application of, those beliefs. His demand that actors be wholly professional and his contempt for those who compromised in their standards were unremitting. He offered as his models and ideals not only Molière and Ruzante but also unsung actors who played Harlequin or had been clowns and performers of cabaret. The motivation behind laughter has long engaged his interest, and is a topic discussed with growing regularity in his talks, including in the speeches in Stockholm when he received the Nobel Prize.

His ideal theatre is dissident, comic, satirical, written with inventive spirit and performed with brio, often with the writer in the main role. After the anonymous jesters of the Middle Ages, the first actor-author recognised by Fo is Ruzante, while instances of the figure in subsequent centuries include the *capocomico* of *commedia dell'arte*, the nineteenth-century *mattattore* (the contemporary and approximately the equivalent of the actor-manager of Anglo-American theatre) and more recently such figures in Neapolitan theatre as Eduardo Scarpetta and Eduardo De Filippo. From the outset, Fo has performed his own work and on those very rare occasions when he has used the work of other writers, has transformed it so deeply that it becomes his own. This is true even of *Dario Fo Plays Ruzante*, premiered in Spoleto in 1993, the homage piece Dario wrote and presented on the actor-author whom he admires above all others.

In spite of suffering a stroke in 1995 which affected his memory and eyesight, Dario has never stopped writing and performing. He has developed a variation of the one-man play which can be called the lecture-performance, where he performs and speaks with the aid of graphs, slides and illustrations. Due to the after effects of the stroke, he also requires the presence onstage of a prompter who has the thankless task of following a script which had been prepared in advance but which Dario would blithely ignore as he improvised his way through his subject. However, his memory was liable to suddenly dry up and he would turn to the prompter for a cue to allow him to carry on. In modern society as a whole, his real prompters in recent years have been an incongruous quartet made up of the widely differing figures of Silvio Berlusconi, Matteo Renzi, Beppe Grillo and Pope Francis. The first two have sharpened his polemical and satiric bent, and the second two encouraged his faltering optimism.

Chapter 2

WHEN YOU ARE SOMEBODY

In 1933, one year before he was awarded the Nobel Prize and three years before his death, Luigi Pirandello wrote a wry, introspective, unquestionably autobiographical play, *Quando si è qualcuno*, (When You Are Somebody) which addressed, among other things, the perils and discontents of fame. The central character is identified only as "Somebody" and the dialogue spoken by him is indicated in the script not by a name but by a series of asterisks. Once a celebrated poet, he has fallen out of fashion and suffers the indignity of seeing himself dismissed with slighting words by a new generation of critics who prefer a new voice, Délago. In an age when celebrity journalism was emerging, this new writer has remained curiously unsighted, but it transpires that Délago is in fact the older poet who has decided not simply to use a pseudonym but to invent for himself, in accordance with a very Pirandellian philosophy, a new identity and personality. In an odd confirmation of the work's central thesis, Pirandello's play failed to find an Italian company willing to stage it and it was premiered in Spanish in Buenos Aires. A Hispanic Pirandello was born to co-exist alongside the established Italian writer.

Having won the Nobel Prize, Dario Fo became unquestionably Somebody, facing the problems and challenges accompanying this status, although they were of a different order from those confronting Pirandello's protagonist. Dario had long been accustomed to fame and universal recognition, but there was now attributed to him a new prestige which came accompanied by some of the other aspects of the process of ageing, physical as well as philosophical. In As You Like It, the doleful philosopher, Jaques, lists the seven ages of man from infancy to old age, the last being the period when the elderly human being takes on the persona of the "lean and slippered Pantaloon." Among characters of commedia dell'arte, Dario had always preferred the Venetian stock character Harlequin to the Neapolitan

Pantaloon, and in the 1990s he was no longer the lean, lanky figure he had been in his youth. In contemporary society, it would be proper to add, at least for those figures who attain the modern condition of "celebrity", another state to Jaques' seven. In English, it is a status known as that of the Grand Old Man (GOM), an honour granted to those who had been at the centre of public polemics in youth but who reach in maturity a temperate zone where controversy is no longer courted, and where in consequence criticism is muted and grudging respect accorded even by those who had been tenacious opponents of every move the GOM had previously made. In this gentler zone, reputation is secure provided certain conventions are respected. This stage in life is normally accompanied by a loss of energy and creativity on the part of the subject, a display of perhaps grudging acceptance of the prevailing status quo and a consequent decline of interest in advocating social or political change as it affects those who will inhabit society after the Somebody has left the stage.

On a superficial view, it would appear that in the years following the award of the Nobel Prize, Dario and Franca were accorded respect of this sort. They were now the regular recipients of honours, prizes and awards in Italy and abroad. In 1998, immediately after the Nobel ceremony, the French Ministry of Culture made Dario a Commendateur des Arts et des Lettres, and both he and Franca were given honorary citizenship of many Italian towns, including Pieve Emanuele, Cesenatico and Riolo Terme, while Dario alone was given this honour in Sartirana Lomellina, where his mother was born. He was also given the gold medal by the Centro Pio Manzú, while Franca received in Spain the Leon Felipe Prize for Human Rights. The Province of Milan awarded her a Gold Medal of Recognition for her work with prisoners and drug addicts. In subsequent years, the couple received jointly or singly honorary degrees from prestigious universities from Harvard to Athens, including Westminster, Sorbonne, Brussels and Santiago de Chile. They had theatres named after them and festivals organised in their honour; were awarded literary and theatrical prizes, were the subject of retrospectives, were invited to many countries to give lectures or make personal appearances and received sufficient medals and plaques in gold to pay off the debts of a small African state. To their occasional embarrassment, they were the subject of academic conferences, the most grandiloquently titled of which was held in Greece in 2000 with the modest title "From Aristophanes to Dario Fo." They found the doors of Italy's RAI and other TV studios open to them, and were also contacted regularly by the international media to make pronouncements on a range of topics on which they had no special expertise. Perhaps most astonishingly of all, after decades in which parish priests had refused them the use of church premises and the Vatican had pronounced anathemas against them for blasphemy and profanity, Dario, particularly in his view of his four plays featuring St Francis of Assisi, received a commendation from the Catholic press in Italy for keeping theological debate alive and for treating religious topics more seriously than many so-called Catholic authors.

Certainly, it was not all sweetness and light and Franca once remarked with some bitterness, and with some exaggeration, "they always criticise us." In all these circumstances it would have been easy, with advancing years and considering the debilitating effects of the stroke he had suffered, for Dario to retire to a life of gilded and respected ease, but he must be included in a special category of those whose energy does not diminish as they age, whose passion is unspent, whose creativity is not impaired, whose curiosity is still keen and whose interest in the manners, mores and ethics of life lose nothing of their sharpness. There are artists, Picasso and Strindberg being obvious examples, who did their best work in what should have been the years Jaques described as being "sans everything". Dario has frequently referred with uncomprehending disbelief to Shakespeare's retirement from the London stage and withdrawal to his birth place of Stratford-Upon-Avon when The Tempest had shown that he was still at the height of his powers. Actors die on stage, he has said, adducing the example of Molière. Listeners have the impression that Dario himself hopes to meet his end in this way. In spite of the testimony of all the Bard's biographers, he has refused to believe that Shakespeare did in fact retire unbidden. "There must have been other forces at work," he has said darkly on more than one occasion.

In his later years, Dario has been drawn to pay literary debts and pay homage to illustrious predecessors in the theatre, Molière and Ruzante in particular. He has promised a book on Shakespeare, who has always intrigued him and on whom his views can be described as showing idiosyncratic fascination. Dario's criticism of other writers is essentially egocentric. He examines them from his own point of view, taking from them what he needs and tending to remake them in his own image and likeness. He searches in Shakespeare for signs of political dissidence, for dissatisfaction with the Elizabethan or Stuart monarchy or with the prevailing status quo and clings to the belief that Shakespeare and his company were persecuted in England precisely because they were players. He had read somewhere that one of the first acts of King James on arrival in London was to expel Shakespeare from the city, and remained sceptical when told that the company in fact performed in court and were given by the new monarch the title The King's Men. Conversely he was fascinated when he learned that Queen Elizabeth had stated, "Richard II is me," fearful that the fate of the deposed monarch in Shakespeare's play was what some of her adversaries had in mind for her. Dario was encouraged by the notion that Shakespeare might have been numbered among such adversaries and that he and his company may have been supporters of the Essex rebellion. In the same tone, he wrote in a recent article that the duel between Laertes and Hamlet and the multiple deaths that follow from it are an allegory. "What is the allegory underlying that slaughter? It is clear. All the rulers in Denmark (but in all truth, the allusion is to the Kingdom of England) deserve to be killed, cancelled from history."[1] Hostility to authority is the position he expects actors and playwrights to demonstrate in their work. Molière and the actors of commedia dell'arte in Paris provide him with an ideal in this respect.

Dario is not cut out to attain the status of a GOM. On the contrary, he has taken to producing works in areas and on topics which are calculated to create dissent, some times from people who were previously sympathetic to his views or had shown no previous interest in them. His intellectual inquisitiveness has expanded into unexpected areas. Although his researches in art history and in biology were thorough and genuine, he was, at least in the latter field, a dilettante, and the spirit in which his research work was carried out and conveyed can be defined as Puckish rather than scholarly. He chooses the path less trodden, moving into a fresh poetic space, assuming a didactic role while avoiding pedantry, taking on the persona of question-master or disseminator of knowledge whose honourable goal is to deepen general consciousness and rearrange the lumber cluttering the mental universe of the populace. His detestation of today's meagre cultural diet of football, tabloid misinformation and TV spectaculars is profound. Fo expresses a view, akin to Nietzsche's by confluence rather than by influence, of the benefits of, or even need for, an aesthetic vision permeating life. Future critics will debate which phase of his life and creativity represents his most significant contribution to Italian theatre, art, politics, society or culture, but it is beyond doubt that there has been no diminution of his energies or closure of his interests. He himself has advanced the view that in his final phase he is doing his most important work. Perhaps. He may now be able to address a wider audience, and irritate more people since the award of the Nobel conferred on him an authority he had not previously enjoyed in Italy, but that is not quite the same thing. The Italian press are in the habit of referring to him as 'the Nobel' without further qualification. He has authored an enormous quantity of books, five in one year, dealing with topics which might have been touched on in previous years, but only tangentially. Subjects he has written on with surprising frequency are the sacred and the erotic.

It is tempting to compare him to an alchemist-scholar of other times, seated at his desk, surrounded by assistants, doing sketches for paintings, turning out books and filmed material which face, with levity, wit and varying degrees of profundity, intriguing problems of life and art. The Fo home in Milan became an atelier, with secretaries, researchers and clerks peopling the offices and rooms, helping in the way apprentices assisted, one must assume, in the bottega of some late Renaissance artist. A monograph on Leonardo's Last Supper was illustrated by two sketches by Dario showing Verrocchio's workshop. The first carries the caption Verrocchio magister and shows two men preparing paint in a large canister, two apprentices examining a canvas while another is seated at a table staring at blocks of wood. The second shows a male model on a pedestal, a figure named as Leonardo contemplating a huge canvas, while others named as Perugino, Botticelli, Lorenzo di Credi and Pollaiolo are perched on a scaffold with brushes in their hands near the same canvas.[2] If the structures are different, the same level of activity surrounds Fo. The intensity of work has taken a toll on his assistants and the turnover among them has been high. The phenomenon of broadcasting would have astonished even the most prescient of alchemists, but Dario has known how to make full use of it alongside the traditional printed word. In the "lecture-performance" genre, ideas are processed from the printed book to stage performance and onto the screen. In this format, he has, in addition to the work on the Last Supper, written and "performed" rather than lectured histories on the Cathedral in Modena and on the city of Ravenna as well as on the masters of the Renaissance he most admires: Giotto, Correggio, Caravaggio, Mantegna, Raphael, and Michelangelo.

This burst of critical writing on Italian artists did not exclude other work. In a late sonnet On His Blindness, the English poet John Milton spoke of his fear of dying before his pen had given expression to all the ideas in his 'teeming brain'. In their later years, Dario and Franca seemed engaged in a similar race against time. It is not possible to subject to critical examination all the works produced in the period post 1997, but their number and range is impressive. Franca's role in this explosion of productivity, apart from the political activity which saw her elected to the senate in Rome, is important. On almost all the recent volumes, it is noted that they were "edited by Franca Rame." This is in one sense unremarkable but is in another sense a recognition not always previously afforded her of her contribution to the output of the couple. Her health was often frail, but she spent hours in front of the computer screen typing, correcting, transcribing, even translating (as in the case of the dialect in the work on Boccaccio) and producing a version of earlier works, Accidental Death of an Anarchist, for example, which will be as definitive as any Fo-Rame work can be. She was also credited with editing the transformation of Can't Pay? Won't Pay! (1974) into a version updated in the light of the 2008 economic crisis as Low Pay? Won't Pay! The play was re-written and directed by Dario for a tour in Italy in 2008, and performed by different companies in Britain and Ireland in 2010. It was Franca who prepared new editions complete with video of such other work as Ruzante and Arlecchino, which came out in 2011 and 2012 respectively as volume and video[3].

Only those who are Somebody are permitted to write an autobiography, and Dario's autobiographical work, Il paese dei mezarat: I miei primi sette anni (e qualcuno in più) was published by Feltrinelli in 2002, appearing in English in 2006 as My First Seven Years (plus a few more).[4] The choice of timescale is based on the principle supposedly enunciated by Bruno Bettelheim that developments in a human being's first seven years are decisive and formative although, as the section in brackets indicates, the book stretches the range of years to include an account of his wartime experiences. In 2004, together with the actor Giorgio Albertazzi he prepared for television Il teatro in Italia, a history of theatre which was left uncompleted when RAI decided to broadcast the programme after midnight. The presenters then decided the game was not worth the candle. This work is wider in scope than the title suggests and opens with an analysis of Greek theatre, moving on to Roman writers and actors, and then examining commedia dell'arte and Renaissance authors. Since the programmes were an invitation to deepen appreciation and enjoyment, critical content was not high. Discussion took in theatre sites as well as acting styles, and it is a matter for regret that the series was broken off.

A celebration of the history of masks, particularly those created by the Sartori family, was prepared as a lecture-performance in the spa town of

Abano Terme in 2005 at the opening of a museum devoted to the Sartoris, and was subsequently broadcast. Other works were conceived as books but the material was then used for on-stage performance, and/or distributed in DVD format, a process made easier by the association he formed with Franco Cosimo Panini publishers, who produced accompanying elegant volumes richly illustrated with paintings by old masters and by Fo himself. These include works on art history, considered in a later chapter, as well as works which look at aspects of religious culture.

Religious issues intrigued him. He is not on the well trodden path from atheism in youth to belief in age, but he does display that greater seriousness of mind described by Montaigne as one of the facets of human ageing and that can carelessly be mistaken for the acquisition of wisdom. Quotations which appear in the introduction to a book on Boccaccio, the first from the Fool in King Lear and the second from Herodotus, could stand for his state of mind. Dario invariably quotes from memory, making hard to find the original, if there is an original. In reply to King Lear's question of why he had fallen into a trap of his own construction, the Fool's avers that he had lived his life in too much haste and had failed to savour "the sublime imbecility of youth." This might be a reference to the Fool's words in Act 2 scene1 to Lear, "thou shouldst not have been old till thou hadst been wise," but it might not. Describing the flight from Halicarnassus, Herodotus wondered why human beings consider only the things which bring success, satisfaction and pleasure, while burying too quickly all that has produced despair and is linked to a deep sense of failure. Fo himself comments that "good and bad luck take each other by the hand like two sisters. If we divide them and exalt only those things which it is convenient to consider, we reduce ourselves to empty beings like forgotten bagpipes."[5] His view of culture and the role played by religion in forming the good life took in both aspects, a celebration of the headlong folly of youth as well as reflections on the darker side of life.

His view of religion expressed in these years is respectful but certainly not devotional. Rizzoli was the publisher of Gesú e le donne (2007, Jesus and Women), a large, sprawling album which relies on the apocryphal gospels, to which Fo had turned on many occasions, as well as on the officially recognised books of the New Testament.[6] The original inspiration was given by a visit Dario and Franca made to Barcelona to perform in the teatre grec. The group on stage before them were gypsy singers who sang that "Christ was undoubtedly a gypsy," and that he "snapped his fingers and danced." No one was able to identify the author of this number which probably belonged to folklore, but discussions and research led the couple to reconsider the role of women in the life of Christ and to mount in this book an attack on institutional or religious-based misogyny. The book is lavishly illustrated with some cartoons by Dario, as well as reproductions of mosaics in Ravenna and of Renaissance masterpieces.

The same theme is developed in L'amore e lo sghignazzo (Love and the Guffaw), published in the same year, and containing five tales of utopian dreamers, heretics or transgressives. The first is Héloise, who recounts from her banishment in Argenteuil the story of her forbidden love for Abélard, while another is Mainfreda of the Milanese noble family, the Visconti, who renounced her position in society and took the veil but was disturbed by the low esteem in which women were held by the church. "A woman is worth exactly as much as a man, so we women in this community are not willing to submit neither to husband or priest."[7] Exactly as he had done with political topics, Fo searched history for examples of women's suppression, and made stories from his research.

Perhaps only Fo could twine together religious and erotic elements, as he did in two books published in 2010, La Bibbia dei villani (The Peasants' Bible) and L'osceno è sacro (The Obscene is Sacred). The first is a further expression of his scrutiny of popular culture, specifically of the social-political vision inherent in the popular beliefs and cults related to Christianity. To that extent, The Peasants' Bible can be regarded as an extension of the thinking which produced Mistero buffo. He was invited by the canons of St. Paul's Outside the Walls in Rome to prepare a lecture-performance to celebrate and publicise the Bible of the French King Charles the Bald which is in the possession of the basilica. In the event, the performance was premiered in Benevento in 1996, but Fo continued working on the idea over the years, coming across bibles of different sorts with "stories in opposition to official Bibles, stories which derive from written and oral tradition in every region of Italy." The quest for popular alternatives to conventional tradition, what Gramsci termed the hegemonic line, was Dario's equivalent of the search for the Holy Grail. He spent much of his life searching, and then embellishing, enhancing, making accessible and at times inventing, aspects of a culture, a people's culture, which he was convinced existed underground and which had been ignored, perhaps systematically, by the protectors and exponents of the dominant cultural tradition. Popular culture is to be located in the by-ways of religious celebrations, in the writings, hymns, feasts and cults which were had been written out of history and were now denied official recognition but which had been an intrinsic element of popular devotion. As he wrote of the peasants' bibles:

> (It is) moving to witness the affectionate attitude of God towards every creature, especially towards peasants. Splendid is the image of God which peasants have. Peasants never think of reducing God to the level of man, not even if that man is an emperor, or of raising themselves to the level of God. For them God is immense, vague and infinitely great, stretched out on the seas or on the mountains. He rolls on the clouds and every so often peeps out to see his creation. "Oh what a beautiful universe I have set up! Look, what a masterpiece that animal is! And that one too! A horse! How lovely a horse is!"

This God, as Fo reports the peasants' belief, is the opposite of the Manichean divinity. He does not recognise the distinction between the spiritual and material dimensions, and this allows peasants to spurn any notion that material things or beings are in some way inferior. Dario writes on their behalf that

> God is in a jug of wine or in the lamb that they are slaughtering. The peasants have always been eating God. They love and they curse him. They are sure that God is goodness but also in part evil, that he is the father of the angels but also a near relative of the devils, that he is life but is also death.[8]

The God of the peasantry can also be female, as the lavish illustrations in the book, assert. The cover shows a naked woman, the Great Mother, with a torch and a dove in each of her raised hands and two goats sucking from each of her breasts. The chapters, sketches in the performance version, begin with the story, unrecorded in Genesis, of the creation of the pig, and then retell many of the dramatic incidents narrated in the Old and New Testaments, such as Adam and Eve, Cain and Abel, Sodom and Gomorra as well as such later episodes as the Slaughter of the Innocents and the scene of Mary standing under the cross on which her son is being crucified.

If the sacred was a new interest, the erotic, if not exactly the obscene, had always figured in Dario's creativity, but it is viewed from a fresh angle in *The Obscene is Sacred,* an interesting work which brings together several of Fo's interests at this time.[9] Fo always had the insight and artistic flair to bring implausible opposites into arresting juxtaposition with the aim of displaying unconsidered truths about both, although that is a trick he does not really pull off in this work. The two poles of the antithesis are never quite reconciled in a convincing synthesis. In spite of the grand title, it is not a treatise of the sort Walter Benjamin might have attempted. Once again, sections of the book were performed as a one-man show. Fo's on-stage work has always been offered in the most varied styles, but his principal theatrical personae are as actor-author and teller of tales. The narration was embellished by the actor's skills, delicate or clownish gestures, graceful or graceless gyrations of the body, grimaces, roars, expressions of disbelief and modulations of voice. Once again, as was common in this phase of his life, the book was embellished by copious original illustrations done by Fo himself, many of which are sexy, sexually explicit, raunchy, or voluptuous, featuring naked females or couples in positions of joyous, uninhibited intimacy. No man has less of the pinched, repressed puritan in his make-up. Sexual humour is everywhere in evidence. Some are inspired by classical works while others are original creations of Fo's imagination, some are basic line drawings and others elaborately worked and coloured paintings.

The opening illustration is a detail of a painting by Correggio, on whom Fo had previously produced a monograph, showing a naked male figure suspended in the clouds as he watches the Assumption of the Virgin. The painting itself is in the cupola of the cathedral in Parma, and the male is seen from below, legs apart, genitals in full view. Other illustrations scattered through the work depict scenes from Ovid, priestesses at the temple of Venus and a recumbent female in the style of a Titian Venus in a coloured sketch entitled *Still Life with Female Nude and Fruit*. Among many other reproductions and illustrations, there are incidents from the *Arabian Nights*, carvings on Hindu temples and the amorous encounters of Hercules once he had completed his more exacting labours. St Ambrose is also there due to his intention to establish a unisex religious community, although the women are in this case modestly clad. St Francis, who was a recurring presence in Fo's output, was pressed into service because before his conversion he had loved women and "dedicated to them love ballads in Provencal." None are extant.

Fo is half way through *The Obscene is Sacred* before he clarifies that the topic he wishes to examine is that of "language and behaviour in regard to the erotic." In fact the range is much wider. The opening sections do consider in detail various words, in dialect and the national language, for the sexual organs. The obscene, he asserts, is part of daily life, and only the censorious power of church and state had suppressed the rumbustiously liberated language used by the people to describe sexual activity. Fo's writing is free of all gravitas or solemnity, but as with his Nobel Prize speech, under the surface there lurks a seriousness of purpose. That is not to say that all his assertions would withstand scrutiny, but he joyfully plunders passages from *Hamlet*, as well as stories from Neapolitan folklore, traditional tales of Pulcinella's travels to the moon to demonstrate the liberated promiscuousness of mind that has been lost. As he proceeds, he retells the story of *The Butterfly Mouse*, which had already featured in his one-man *Obscene Fables* (1981), where the butterfly mouse is the vagina which has unfortunately run off, or so the conniving female in the tale tells her ingenuous husband, whom she has married only to avoid the awkwardness of admitting that she is pregnant by her priest-lover. The new husband is dispatched to find it, leaving her to devote her attention to her lover. A large part of the remainder of the book is taken up with a retelling of some of the more alluring and mischievous tales told by Scheherazade.

Only at a very late stage does the sacred come into play, and even then somewhat summarily. Dario refers to an unnamed American researcher who had found that in the Orient the spot where some act of violence occurred could be cleansed by rituals involving groups of people, clowns and "comic elephants" who recount humorous tales and perform "obscene acts and fictitious violence." In the Christian tradition, he refers to liturgical acts, the *Exultet* and *Risus Paschalis*, once performed in church at Easter, and which could reach a climax with singing and dancing. Sometimes these practices got out of hand and so were suppressed. An illustration on a red background featuring naked couples in positions suggests a loss of composure and clarifies the reason for the clerical veto.

A renewed interest in story-telling and in the erotic was bound to lead Dario to Giovanni Boccaccio, Italy's most renowned teller of tales and one who was not averse to narratives with a high erotic content. *Il Boccaccio riveduto e scorretto* (A Revised and Incorrect Boccaccio – although the Italian *scorretto* is an untranslatable pun which can mean both "uncorrected" as well "incorrect") was published in 2011 and is a personal reconsideration of a writer whom Fo had earlier dismissed as reactionary. In the new evaluation, Boccaccio is presented and celebrated not only as a short-story writer of genius and as a neglected humanist thinker, but as a man who had advocated living life to the full, in line with the beliefs of Herodotus and Lear's Fool. Many of his protagonists had luxuriated fully in all the opportunities life offered the rebellious, hedonist young, even in the midst of the calamity of the plague which drove his story-tellers from Florence in the first place. In the stories which make up the *Decameron*, Fo detects that combination of the tragic and the farcical which was his personal ideal in drama, but which was, he writes, a revolutionary innovation introduced by Boccaccio, and one which made possible the emergence of *commedia dell'arte* and which influenced Shakespeare. Dario is not given to cautious or measured judgments. As he writes:

> Briefly, without this free alteration of the balance of narrative, we would not have had the advantage of the great revolution of *commedia dell'arte* and, following from that, of the extraordinary renovation of all European theatre starting with the Elizabethans; led by Shakespeare.[10]

Fo provides both a guide to Boccaccio and a retelling of many of the tales. He begins with the story of Ginevra, which provided one element of the plot of Shakespeare's *Cymbeline*, although he did not exactly "translate" it as Fo suggests. The ending of the tale, where in the court of the Sultan Ginevra pardons the husband who had commissioned a friend to kill her in vengeance for an adultery she had not committed, did not satisfy Fo any more than the similar ending of Cymbeline had pleased Bernard Shaw. Quoting Shaw as justification for his alterations to the ending, Fo has Ginevra say that she would prefer to remain as a concubine in the sultan's court rather than return to the marital home. It is not clear how exactly this new ending represents an improvement of women's lot.

Among the qualities Fo praises in Boccaccio are his willingness to condemn himself as a plagiarist or even an outright thief of stories created by other writers, a crime of which Fo himself was often cheerfully guilty. More impressive was Boccaccio's willingness to base some tales on events and characters who really existed, since this was a demonstration of his critical observation of aspects of contemporary society. In his presentation of the doings of the usurer, the first story on Day One of the original *Decameron*, Fo deplores the growth of the banking industry in early Renaissance Italy. He also notes the central position Boccaccio gives to women, either as narrator or protagonist. "One of the great achievements of Boccaccio is to have given prime place ... to the female world, making women often absolute interpreters of the story-performance." Fo permits himself considerable leeway in his retelling of some of the other thirteen tales he narrates, but they are all recounted with brio and panache.

Meantime, he produced two books written in conjunction with the journalist Giuseppina Manin. The first, *Il mondo secondo Fo* (2007, The World According to Fo), an interview in which Fo reminisces on his life in the theatre. It was followed by *Il paese dei misteri buffi* (2012, The Town of the Comic Mysteries), which consists of a series of sketches on Italian public life in an, obviously, satirical vein. The characters featured were mainly politicians from the First Republic, with Berlusconi as undisputed protagonist. To this list, which is incomplete, could be added works of a generally scientific interest, where the science is viewed from the perspective of a moralist. *L'apocalisse rimandata* (The Apocalypse Postponed, 2008) is an ecological tract and the DVD *Dio è nero* (God is Black), originally delivered at the Museum of Natural History in Milan on Evolution Day, 2011, takes a sideways look at Darwinism. Evolution is viewed idiosyncratically in an imaginary dialogue, where the central topic is the appearance of human life in Africa, and the twist is that since man is made in the likeness of God, God must be black. The lecture moves beyond biology to reprise ideas advanced elsewhere on the coming ecological catastrophe when resources run out, and concludes with the hope of a return to an original, gentler matriarchy. One of the highlights was Dario's delighted reply to a young boy who asked, "How do you become primitive?"

Dario had also been invited over the years to direct several operas. The first was a thoroughly revised version of Stravinsky's *Histoire du soldat* at the Piccolo in 1978. Increasingly he was attracted to Rossini, and worked on several occasions at the Rossini Festival in Pesaro, the composer's home town. He directed *The Barber of Seville* in Amsterdam in 1987, and later *The Italian Girl in Algiers*, produced in both Amsterdam and Pesaro in 1994. *La Gazzetta* was produced at the Festival in 2001, *Il Viaggio a Reims* staged in Helsinki in 2003 and later in Genoa, and a new production of *The Barber of Seville* in Catania in 2010. These productions were controversial and offended many conventional music and opera critics, since Dario re-imagined and re-created these works in his own idiosyncratic style, focusing more on acting and scenery than on music. His maim aim was to present Rossini as belonging to the tradition of *commedia dell'arte*. Some critics were accommodating in their response. Watching Dario take command of every aspect of production, a dazzled journalist in *Sipario* observed: "There is no lack of actor-directors, but they stage the works of other writers; nor of author-directors; nor of actor-authors, but I have no recollection of actor-designers, much less of actor-playwright-director-designer-costumiers..."[11]

REFERENCES

1   *Il Fatto Quotidiano*, 7 December 2013.

2   Dario Fo, *Lezione sul cenacolo di Leonardo*, San Lazzaro di Savena, Nuovi Mondi edizioni, 2001, p.33. Second edition, revised and extended, Modena, Franco Cosimo Panini, 2007.

3   Dario Fo, *Hellequi Harlekin Arlekin Arlecchino*, edited and translated by Franca Rame, Turin, Einaudi, 2011. Dario Fo and Franca Rame, *Ruzzante*, Turin, Einaudi, 2012.

4   Dario Fo, *Il paese dei mezarat: i miei primi sette anni(e qualcuno in più)*, Milan, Feltrinelli, 2992; English translation by Joseph Farrell, *My First Seven Years (plus a few more)*, London, Methuen, 2005.

5   Dario Fo, edited by Franca Rame, *Il Boccaccio riveduto e scorretto*, Parma, Guanda, 2011, p.8

6   Dario Fo, *Gesú e le donne*, Milan, Rizzoli, 2007.

7   Dario Fo, *L'amore e lo sghignazzo*, Parma, Guanda, 2007, p.64.

8   Dario Fo, *La Bibbia dei villani*, Parma, Guanda, 2010, pp 11, 14.

9   Dario Fo, *L'osceno è sacro*, Parma, Guanda, 2010.

10   *Il Boccaccio riveduto e scorretto*,, cit, p16.

11   Domenico Manzella, quoted by Christopher Cairns in *Dario Fo e la "pittura scenica"*, Naples, Edizioni Scientifiche Italiane, 2000, p. 131

Chapter 3

"OBSERVE AND READ WITH ME": ARTIST AND ART HISTORIAN

❝❝ I have been painting ever since I was a boy," said Dario when inter-
viewed before the opening of an exhibition of his work in Pontedera
in 2010. "I began before learning how to form numbers. I was quite
good, a little phenomenon," he said cheerfully.[1] In the autobiographical
My First Seven Years, he recalls occasions when in his home town of Valtravaglia he was invited to paint the portraits of schoolmates or townspeo-
ple, including his teacher, the daughters of the mayor and the mistress
of a gangland boss. "More than one enthusiastic parent repaid me with
gifts, some with cash." On one occasion, he received a commission to do
portraits of a farmer's family, for which he was recompensed by the gift
of a large dog which he named Gog. He grew to love this dog but it caused
havoc with the sheep and was eventually hunted down by local shepherds.
Given this innate talent and artistic background, it might seem paradoxical to suggest that there was something novel about Dario's absorption in
art, art criticism and art history from the late 1990s onwards, but he had
become identified in Italy and abroad as a man of theatre so his return
to the visual arts undoubtedly represented a reordering of priorities. In
part, this was a response to his conditions of health after suffering the
stroke. His eyesight was poor and reading and writing were difficult, but
he was able to paint new work, to create figures, to reproduce and re-im-
agine the works of other artists and above all to produce a commentary on
their canvases as well as on his own times.

This new dedication to painting took the double form of an outburst
of personal creative activity and an absorption in the history of art. Dario had never undertaken an academic or systematic study of drama. In
his youth in Milan in the 1940s, he studied art and architecture at the
Brera and at the Politecnico, and in the heightened cultural frenzy of Milan in the period following the Liberation, his intellectual focus was on

artistic not theatrical activity: "I knew De Chirico, I was in contact with Carlo Carrà, as well as with Ennio Morlotti, Emilio Tadini, Bruno Cassinari, Cesare Peverelli, Alik Cavaliere. I also met Remo Brindisi and many others later." He added that he went to Paris where he had got to know Léger "quite well," but perhaps two seemingly more casual assertions made in a revealing interview in 1984 were more important: firstly, that he was "passionate about the Renaissance, not only the Italian Renaissance but also the Spanish Renaissance. I studied the Flemish and French Great Masters," and secondly that he had "always had a predilection for representational art."[2] His preference for the representational style was evident in his own work from the beginning, while his statement of love for Renaissance artists determined those whose work he would celebrate in the period of his life under discussion, whether on stage, in TV programmes or in books. After an initial lecture-performance on Leonardo in 2001, he launched himself on a new career as art historian, critic and populariser. He was no debunker. The objective of his criticism was illumination, the main driving force was admiration, the main response to the artists he discussed was delight and the main ambition a desire to share that admiration and delight. This love for certain Renaissance artists can be seen as a parallel to his quest in theatre in the late sixties into medieval theatre, leading to *Mistero buffo*. Fo's habitat is tradition, but his instincts are popularising.

His writings on art in the 1990s and beyond indicate a new scale of human and humanist values, a wider vision of the individual and society, founded on the recognition that political engagement and the values of cultural life taken together are the twin requisites of civilisation, in any epoch. He had moved at an earlier phase of zeal for exclusively political activity to an involvement in social causes, but now his thinking showed evidence of a heightened awareness of the need for the deepening and dissemination of cultural and artistic values. When writing of the artists of the Renaissance, Fo addressed himself to those who had been traditionally excluded from the appreciation and enjoyment of art by the restrictive language employed by scholars and experts. There is something in his viewpoint which brought him close to John Ruskin, although there is no reason to believe he had any familiarity with the Englishman's writings.

His criticism of art and artists could be described as a venture in erudite populism. He made use of political categories and judgements, but not in the style of Marxist critics of earlier generations. His objective was to lay bare the workings of the hierarchies of power in the production of art, but he was not out to present cultural products merely as self-serving, hegemonic dressing imposed by the rich and powerful to justify or embellish the sordid substructure or the glitzy superstructure of society. For Fo the ethical, aesthetic and philosophical complex of values which go under the name 'culture' was principally a force which enhanced life and represented a higher value in itself. He deplored the fall in educational standards and the coarsening of culture, especially popular culture, in contemporary society, so when discussing Michelangelo in his lecture-show, he outlined the view of education and culture held by rulers then with the situation today: "in the sixteenth century even despots understood the importance of a cultured citizenry, and knew that an ignorant population is something negative. They also understood the value of the individual citizen with knowledge, even if that involved the risk of them wanting to participate in government."[3] The point of comparison with the degraded civilisation of today was left unstated. More than once, he compared the reaction to the unveiling of works of art in Florence or Rome to the crowds now who now flocked to football stadiums, or the willingness of princes and dukes to gather artists in their courts in Urbino, Mantua or Ferrara to the keenness of contemporary European plutocrats to purchase footballers for the teams they owned. As a democrat and a utopian, Fo was motivated by a desire to share all that was good. He was not moving into the field of high art as it was commonly understood, but was intent on indicating the presence of the popular even among the old masters commonly identified, in the division of cultural spheres theorised by Antonio Gramsci, as belonging to the hegemonic tradition.

The invitation by the Minister for Culture, Giovanna Melandri, to deliver a speech on 27 May 1999 at the unveiling of the restored *Last Supper* represented a change in the official attitude towards Dario.[4] The government was a left-wing coalition headed by Massimo D'Alema, with Silvio Berlusconi in opposition. Melandri was American by birth but Italian by upbringing, and in fact held dual citizenship. She rose to prominence as an environmental activist, and in politics was active in the Left Democrats, a grouping which included most of the ex-members of the Communist party.

Leonardo's masterpiece had started to deteriorate almost as soon as it had been completed, and several attempts had been made in previous centuries to return it to its pristine state. The task of major restoration was entrusted to Pinin Brambilla Barcilon, who dedicated 21 years to the project, four times as long as Leonardo had taken for the original creation of his masterpiece. The restoration work drew heavy criticism in some quarters for its undue boldness, for producing changes in colours and tones and for the loss of all sense of history, but Dario, like Giovanna Melandri was broadly supportive.

His talk was broadcast on Italy's main TV channel. As with his Nobel Prize speech a few years before, beneath the lightness, there was a critical method and an aesthetic. Emilio Tadini in 1984 had called attention to the strength of Fo's visual sense, both in theatre and in painting.

> Dario Fo's theatre has been and continues to be enhanced by his extraordinary capacity to see: it is enhanced, we might say, by his extraordinary ability to make figures, to create figures, to arrange sense and meaning in figures – more precisely, to uncover sense and meaning in the figures.[5]

Tadini, himself a highly regarded artist in Italy, identified in Fo a further "ability to see the unexpected in already famous painters," together with a formidable critical intellect accompanied by love and erudition. These qualities would form the basis of all his writings on art.

The tone was off-hand, light, jaunty and jovial, totally devoid of any dry-as-dust gravitas or solemnity. He recalled times when he had visited the refectory and listened to guides, some learned, some ill-informed, but all focusing on individual figures, or on the grouping of the apostles into three, a number taken to be significant, perhaps in homage to the Trinity or to cabbalistic numbers. Dario was happy to pay homage to the deep religious sense underlying the painting and to discard all notions that Leonardo was a sceptic or even a cynical atheist but as a critic he was more interested in drawing attention to the overall design. His focus in aesthetic terms was on the painterly qualities, the dynamism and sense of theatrical movement in the arrangement of the figures, the choreography of the hands, clothes and even shoes glimpsed under the table and on the general geometric perspective. He relied on Giorgio Vasari's description of Leonardo's modus operandi, especially his account of the construction of special scaffolding which allowed him to work at the level of the faces and to make Christ's right eye the ideal centre of the painting.

The introduction to the subsequent volume is largely biographical and historical, without any attempt at the kind of analysis of the psyche of the artist of the type favoured by Freud. He was intrigued by two coincidences, that Leonardo was born in the same year as Savonarola, and that he was illegitimate, like Ruzante, Fo's favourite actor-author. The Church ensured that illegitimate children were barred from attending institutions of learning, but Dario speculated that such exclusion may have encouraged in Leonardo independence of thought and a preference for experimentation. He ponders other aspects of Leonardo's biography, for instance his friendship with Machiavelli which may have fostered the growth of the democratic spirit, for Fo's Machiavelli is not the amoral worshipper celebrator of naked power he is now believed to be, but primarily a republican democratic.

Democratic he may have been, but at the same time Leonardo was the servant of princes in all fields, one of the contradictions which make him an enigmatic figure whose beliefs and practices are beyond the reach of any modern mindset. For Dario, nothing illustrates these oppositional forces better than the attitude towards war and violence. While imbued with the Humanist vision, Leonardo was uncritical of the warlike nature of his own age. In his notebooks, Fo observes, Leonardo demonstrated a deeply religious, humane spirit, and was moved by the wonder of creation. He described man as indeed the measure of all things, and as such a creature of beauty whom it would be a crime to destroy, yet he had no compunction in developing weaponry of great sophistication. Fo comments, "Italy may be called the cradle of the Renaissance, but it was also called the land of the dead because of the great number of corpses scattered all over the land." Fo was never the pure historian, but preferred to move backwards and forwards from the past to the present, so his speculation about the mentality that allowed Leonardo and other artists such as Verrocchio to devote their genius to developing weaponry borrow from the recently coined vocabulary of "weapons of mass destruction."

Fo expatiates on other works besides the *Last Supper*, showing his own visual acuteness but also his quirkiness of vision. On *La visitazione dei Magi* (The Adoration of the Magi), he draws attention to the dark areas behind the central scene of the Mother and Child and the kneeling visitors, where battles are still underway and women and children flee in terror. "Peace to men of good will," he writes, had not been established. His curiosity, or sense of mischief, was also aroused by a scarcely visible incident where an angel with a long horn is plainly blowing raucously into the ear of a fellow angel who is not grateful for the attention. These grotesque, off-centre scenes will always enlighten and lighten his judgements on the works he will discuss.

His treatment of Leonardo, and of the other artists about whom he will write in these years, is embellished by sketches and paintings of his own.

These may be illustrations of incidents mentioned, for instance, the delegation led by Leonardo to Ludovico Sforza in Milan to deliver the gift of a lyre in the shape of a horse's head. One man, presumably Ludovico, raises his hand to the mouth of the instrument-animal which is being held by another, presumably the artist. In the background are vessels on waters representing the canals which were once as numerous in Milan as those in Venice. On the facing page, there is a portrait of how Leonardo "probably looked when 30 years old." Another painting illustrates the use for target practice of a statue of Francesco Sforza sculpted by Leonardo but treated with disdain by soldiers, an event recorded by Vasari. Other illustrations have a more explicitly didactic purpose. To help explain the perspective of the *Last Supper,* he drew one particularly striking, or outrageous, scene in which a naked figure floats over the head of Christ in "mechanical levitation," to demonstrate Fo's notion of the "scenic totality" of the painting.

Shortly before this lecture, Dario published a history of Ravenna.[6] At the promptings of a group of art students from Ravenna who turned up at his holiday home in Cesenatico to enlist his help for a project they were engaged on, he became engrossed in the history of the city, although the final book devotes as much space to Constantinople, the other capital of the divided Roman Empire, as to the stated subject of the book. It is a work of history, not a discussion of the art or architecture or mosaics in the churches. The period covered goes from the foundation of Ravenna until the arrival of the Longobards in Italy in the sixth century. If it is popular history, written in a conversational, relaxed, whimsical, playful, accessible and occasionally comic style, it is founded on scholarship and knowledge and is not in any sense a spoof attempt to demythologise or lampoon the history of this city.

The book has the appearance of a graphic novel, with original illustrations by Fo of arresting scenes and characters in the history, such as a colourful painting of the journey of the future Empress Theodora to Africa with her rich merchant husband, or pen drawings of Belisarius on horseback or of the love-making of Galla Placidia and Attila, as well as re-elaborations by Fo of the Ravenna mosaics or other classical works. These artworks, neither kitsch nor pastiche, are part of the narrative, an alternative history of Ravenna and Constantinople. Fo does not take any post-modern, relativist view of historical fact, but questions and reproaches contemporary historians for ignoring certain episodes or for presenting them in terms of 'mystification.' Authors quoted range from Procopius in classical times to the modern historian, Pasquale Villari. There is nothing invented in a chronicle which discusses the construction of the aqueduct by Trajan, the need for reinforced wooden poles driven into the ground to provide foundations, the biography of Galla Placidia, the explanation of the Arian heresy, the detailed account of imperial family jealousies and the tormented relations of Theodora and the Emperor Justinian. Granted Fo's outlook, he is also interested in what has *not* changed. This is history seen in the class terms Gramsci would have recognised. Theodora is presented both as a proto-feminist who made her own way in life, working first as a prostitute before later, as empress, closing brothels and locking the women in convents. She also closed theatres, Fo writes, bringing to an end a rich tradition. Justinian is not the codifier of laws who wins a place in Dante's Paradiso, or not only that, but a mass murderer and psychopath. The hero of the piece is the Ostrogoth Totila, who recruited an army of slaves and peasants and redistributed land, believing that every man will fight more tenaciously in defence of his own fields than of a distant ruler. An original illustration by Fo on the battle of Caprara where Totila was finally defeated by the imperial army under Narses, a eunuch of Armenian origin who rose to become a general in the army of Byzantium and who pacified Italy in the interests of Eastern Emperors in Constantinople, carries the caption, with words attributed to Narses himself – "But why do they insist? They are now defeated, but they fight not for king but for their lands." Fo's Totila was a successor of Spartacus, a liberator of peasants and proletarians. In a sign of changed times, the volume received the commendation of the cardinal archbishop of the city.

The most significant and engaging work of this period was probably that on the cathedral in Modena, which in many ways provided the ideal vehicle for the expression of Fo's views of art and history. The work took the form of a televised lecture-performance on the architecture and history of the cathedral and its relations with the city. The programme and the later printed version were given the title, *Il tempio degli uomini liberi* (The Temple of Free Men), as the population of Modena at that time boasted of being.[7] Not all churchmen in Italy had changed their views of him, and he encountered opposition of a more traditional type when he announced the project. The local church reacted in an unthinking style Pavlov would have recognised. Novenas and public recitations of the rosary were organised, all inspired by the fear that Fo would provide a blasphemous, Marxist or atheist interpretation of the pious work of medieval artisans. Paradoxically had they had a deeper knowledge of the mixture of the sacred and secular in medieval, ecclesiastical architecture, they could have spared themselves the trouble.

Fo invited those who attended the spectacle, which was given in the open air outside the cathedral on an extemporised stage with two giant screens on either side of him, to read the architecture as they would read a book. Since the book was medieval, the language would be as unfamiliar as the *Divine Comedy*, but Fo acted as decoder and populariser, obviously performing in his own style, throwing in jokes about contemporary politics and ironic allusions to the present day. Berlusconi could never be too far away. Discussing a carving of the Flood, he remarked: "In the days of Noah, the Eternal Father saw that the world was not to his liking, that there were men in government who made laws in their own interest, and he decided to send the Flood. We can only hope that he doesn't have the same idea today." There was no irony on belief, nor did Fo use the sacred architecture as a pretext for superficial jokes on the naivety of primitive styles of representational art, as Renaissance art historians like Vasari were wont to do. At one point, having just discussed the protection God gave to Cain after his murder of his brother, he digressed into a philippic against violence, but stopped the crowd from applauding. "I prefer your astonishment. That's the right reaction".

Behind the professionalism of the skilled performer, there lies genuine erudition. When dealing with history, whether political, architectural or artistic, Fo is never a bluffer. He may offend experts, his style of delivery may be more appropriate to the entertainer than the meticulous lecturer, but he deals in facts which have been researched and checked. The cathedral was constructed between 1099 and 1117, a time of conflict between Church and Empire over the question of investitures, an issue recounted without the leaven of humour. The Gothic is normally regarded as dating from the later 12th century, and the cathedral, like the art and architecture of the time of construction, bears signs of being designed in an age of transition. St Augustine wrote that ecclesiastical art should aim to be the *libri idiotarum*, the books of the illiterate, and medieval architecture, to whatever phase it is attributed, is an encyclopaedia. Its decorative range stretches well beyond what would conventionally nowadays be regarded as pious art, and it is this aspect that Dario revelled in revealing, perhaps because it confirms what he already believed about medieval culture and what he had discussed when staging *Mistero buffo*. Even before that, he claimed to have learned the nature of popular art by studying the Romanesque churches in out-of-the-way villages in his native Lombardy where he was, he said, impressed by the artistry, sophistication, mastery of technique of unsung and nameless masons and iron workers who would never have claimed to be other than artisans. By nature, he was not given to systematic treatment of any topic, and no man has ever been less given to developing theses, but his approach has, once again, much in common with that of John Ruskin or even Henry Adams in his classic *Mont Saint Michel and Chartres*. Adams wrote: "The church showed strong leanings towards secular poetry and popular tastes. The drama belonged to it exclusively, and the Mysteries and the Miracle plays which were acted under its patronage often contained nothing of religion except the miracle."[8] It is a pity the clergy in Modena were not better informed. Architecture of this variety and the philosophy which underwrites it are a challenge to 21st century notions of theology and of what constitutes appropriate church art.

Dario delighted in underlining the precarious liberty Modena won for itself in those warlike times, and which the people of Modena used to build their own cathedral which was more than a religious centre. He highlights the fact that where it would have been normal for the name of the lord or bishop who commissioned the work to appear on the walls, in Modena it is the architect, Lanfranco, who is celebrated by a plaque on the outside wall behind the altar. In Fo's interpretation, the Duomo of Modena is a work of popular art, expressing the culture, lay as well as religious, of its time but speaking to people of all ages.

Fo drew special attention to the façade decorated with a riot of foliage, gargoyles, mythical or fantastic beasts. He pointed out how the knights of King Arthur feature on the exterior walls alongside Adam and Eve and how *homo selvaticus* finds a place near a twin-bodied but single-headed deer which may represent the dual nature of Christ. There are even erotic carvings of women with generous breasts generously exposed, representing, in Titian's terms, *amor profano*, not *amor sacro*. The erotic in art was another subject to which Fo was dedicating greater attention.

The works on the great Renaissance masters themselves required a different approach, but once again there was nothing of the dilettante in Fo's treatment of Giotto, Caravaggio, Mantegna, Michelangelo, Correggio, Leonardo or Raphael, each the subject of TV documentary and/or a handsomely produced book. His request to his readers or spectators in his discussions of art could be compared Leporello's to Donna Elvira when he is about to show her the list of Don Giovanni's conquests, "oss-ervate, leggete con me," (Observe and read with me).

Fo first encountered Caravaggio in 1948 at an exhibition in the Palazzo Reale in Milan, where he would later exhibit his own work. As he was pre-paring this book, he and Franca came to Edinburgh to present his auto-biography at the Edinburgh Book Festival. They brought with them copi-ous reproductions of Caravaggio, as well as photocopies of excerpts from various works of criticism or history which they spread over the floor of their hotel room, to the dismay of the solicitous staff. Dario was driven around the city to see the castle, the New Town, Holyroodhouse, the ca-thedral of St. Giles and other sights in Scotland's capital, but his attention was elsewhere. Accounts of the history of Parliament House were listened to courteously, but would be followed, disconcertingly, not by requests for elaboration but by a monologue on the Knights of St. John of Mal-ta, thoughts on Caravaggio's time in Sicily or of the dynastic divisions in Rome in the late sixteenth century.

Dario shows no sympathy with conventional, dramatic portraits of the '*artiste maudit*,' preferring to see Caravaggio in the context of the his trou-bled age, so that even the infamous killing of a rival after a game of tennis was, in his view, more probably the result of a political dispute than an act of anger. In more strictly artistic terms, he dismisses those who held that Caravaggio had painted spontaneously, directly on to canvas with no preparation or preparatory sketches, and to support his case makes ref-erence to Carlo Carrà, whom he had known during his student days at the Brera. "Whoever invented this tale of extempore creation? Michelange-lo da Merisi, like his Florentine namesake, was a man who confronted a canvas with everything already in his head and fully imagined."[9] Armed with Carrà's authority, Dario refutes facile notions of Caravaggio's sup-posedly effortless approach, and emphasises the professional artisanship in each of the individual paintings, as well as the painstaking preparatory work needed to give form to his philosophical-theological thought. While many scholars conceal trite thought by the employment of complex, tech-nical vocabulary, Fo employs every-day speech to ensure maximum cur-rency of his analysis. This is more than the "skill in seeing," which Tadini identified, although that is part of it.

He is content to act as unassuming gallery guide as well as informa-tive critic. In reference to *La buona ventura* (The Fortune Teller), he calls attention to "the gesture of the fortune teller," asserting that "with the pretext of reading the line of fortune on the palm of the boy's hand, he is in fact pulling off his ring." This may be an incidental fact, but he subjects *La deposizione nel sepolcro* (The Deposition) to a more detailed, professional examination, illustrating his analysis with the aid of sketches of his own. Victorian art critics, such as John Ruskin when writing on Venetian art, added pen sketches of tombs and church facades, but Fo was not interested in reproduction for its own sake. The sketches in his works serve to illustrate the perspective of the painter or the sight lines from which viewers will see the painting itself. Fuller reproductions often include added figures, or are done with lines and in tones unknown to Renaissance artists, but his illustrations are never pastiches. In other working sketches, he will superimpose geometrical lines, as he had done with Leonardo, to establish Caravaggio as "an authentic mechanic, a scientist of painting." He will also blithely go beyond limits which a professional critic would observe. In his discussion of *San Matteo e l'angelo* (St Matthew and the Angel), he underlines the presence of the "compass and the set square, which he employed for his geometrical developments," but then goes on to interpret the precise message being delivered by the angel. The saint should "liberate himself from theological science so as make the simple doctrine of the humble and poor of spirit his own." Is that Caravaggio's meaning, or Fo's overlay?

Fo's criticism is invariably non-conformist, dictated by his belief in the popular roots evident even in the works of classic great masters. He is forthright in his expressions of contempt for professional art historians, even those of the acknowledged stature of Roberto Longhi or of the historical authority of Giorgio Vasari. He convicts them of the crime of mystification in having made appreciation difficult for those not part of an inner élite, and thus of having betrayed the intention and vision of the artist. Fo's narrative is based on the belief that he is releasing Caravaggio, or Giotto, or whoever, from layers of misunderstanding, and presenting "the real Caravaggio or Giotto". The first characteristic of his criticism is enthusiasm. There is no trace of objectivity or neutrality in his approach to the artists he discusses. Nor are these talks or books the productions of Fo the satirist, except when he implies, subtly, parallels with contemporary society or when he speaks of outrages in history, but such moments are outnumbered by passages of lyrical intensity, expressions of delicacy of feeling or the overwhelming desire to share appreciation and enjoyment. Fo's motivation is love of the painters whose works he surveys, and also a surprising and wholly new level of reverence, evident in, for instance, his discussion of music, of tones of light and shade, of colours of flesh in Caravaggio's *Il riposo durante la fuga in Egitto* (Rest on the Flight into Egypt), and also in Correggio's *L'Assunzione della Vergine* (The Assumption of the Virgin) in the cathedral in Parma. These are works which aroused his awe, and Fo's style in writing and voice carries his admiration.

Increasingly, his approach became idiosyncratic as he chose to highlight the satire, irony and even sarcasm he detected in the attitude and outlook of the painters themselves, particularly so in the case of Mantegna, the subject of, perhaps, the finest of his studies.[10] He had disparaging comments for previous critics of the artist, noting that "the dominant tendency is to look at art for art's sake and not at its different levels; the art of satire, of mockery, or overturning the logic of power, this was not to be studied."[11] It was precisely this aspect that Fo set out to study. He recorded his surprise and pleasure in noting at "all the great artists of every age reserve considerable space in their own works for satirical irony and poetic humour," a tendency he observed in Leonardo, Dante, Giotto. In Mantegna, he found these elements particularly in *I trionfi di Cesare* (The Triumph of Caesar), a series of works commissioned by Francesco II to celebrate his victory over the French at Fornovo. Mantegna devoted more than twenty years to these canvases, and Fo subverts the normal reading by switching the focus from the protagonists to the minor figures. While seemingly fulfilling the commission given by the ruling Gonzaga family, Mantegna made the procession a revelation of the horrors of war, of the emptiness of pomp and of the pettiness of power. One example will suffice. In one canvas, *I Senatori*, Fo draws attention to a boy squeezed between "the buttocks of an obese minister and the belly of a young assistant." What is his function? "A singular motion of sarcastic and at the same time poetic fun which we will learn to uncover and appreciate as we look at the nine works in the series."

The same combination of critical tools is applied to Michelangelo, Raphael and later Correggio.[12] His delight in Correggio seems inspired principally by his admiration for his technical expertise, for instance, in his depiction of the Madonna being assumed into heaven but seemingly light and flying. His narrative shows respect for professional expertise in the composition of the figures in the canvas, reverence and enthusiasm for the artists' beliefs, an eye for the telling but overlooked detail and an ambition to reveal the "true" artist previously concealed by academic interpretations, all with the intention of producing a carefully argued but subversive reading. In Raphael, Fo judges the early works "elegant and delicate", but writes that after he moved to Florence Raphael observed in Florentine painters and sculptors:

> Stories of dramas and festive occasions but also the force of ideas, the indignation against injustice, the violence of those who exercise power, the rage and despairing commitment to see the world change.[13]

The work on Michelangelo contains vivid accounts of his rivalry with Leonardo, as well as beautiful accounts of the Sistine Chapel. There are here more illustrations by Fo himself than in the earlier works.[14]

This new reverence does not prevent him from indulging in a tendency to which he was always prone, that of reinventing artists and writers according to his own convictions. The political dimension is more prominent in Fo's narrative than in other monographs on Renaissance artists. A talk on Giotto was broadcast, after many delays, in 2008 from the Scrovegni Chapel in Padua, where the artist completed in 1305 his celebrated cycle of frescoes of divine history and of the lives of Christ and the Virgin Mary. He viewed Giotto's frescoes as "a mystical, political, and ideological battleground," and detected in them "a painting, a reading against established power."[15] Giotto was in this view a dissident and a rebel against the power used by the Church to impose an interpretation of the Bible which contradicted the social teaching of Christ. Dario noted that Giotto had incorporated scenes from the apocryphal gospels, always a favourite of his. The lecture on Giotto was done to mark the seventh-hundred anniversary of the opening of the Scrovegni chapel, but was also made around the same time as a televised show in Abano Terme to celebrate the opening of a museum of the work of the Sartori family of mask-makers. Since Fo, in disagreement with Vasari, found in Giotto the elegance of Greek art, he was also able to note in both the craft of the Sartori and in the medieval painter a common poetic, a return to myth and to tradition, to the Greeks or to *commedia dell'arte*.

Giotto was then the subject of a fuller lecture in 2009, later published in book form, entitled "Giotto or not Giotto".[16] This occasion was marred by a dispute which pitched the restorer of the cycle of frescoes in the Basilica of St Francis against the bishop of Assisi. Dario took the side of the former in holding that many of the frescos were the work not of Giotto but of the unknown Pietro Cavallini and his assistants. The bishop was annoyed at this heretical belief and withdrew permission to film in the basilica's precincts, so the venue was switched to Perugia. The work was later performed in front to Santa Croce in Florence and at the Politecnico in Milan, but was never broadcast by RAI, seemingly on account of the bishop's objections. There were no further programmes on art history broadcast for a number of years, but Fo continued to publish his criticism.

Sant' Ambrogio e l'invenzione di Milano (2009, Saint Ambrose and the Invention of Milan), suffered from this ban, although it was published at the time and broadcast later.[17] It was in essence a mixture of biography and historical work, similar to his study of the history of Ravenna, and by no means an objective chronicle. It is filled with imagined dialogue and Dario himself makes occasional entries to explain his changing attitudes to his subject. Ambrose is treated not as a devout bishop but as a secular figure prominent in the Roman Empire. Dario tells of his surprise firstly when he discovers that Ambrose owes his rise to prominence to the influential friends he had made, and secondly when he finds no evidence of any conversion or change of heart once Ambrose devoted himself to the church. "How am I to get along with this easy-going "accumulator of offices" who does not show the slightest sign of any crisis of conscience as he intrigues with certain dubious local figures? Is this a Saint?" he was the man who made Milan what it had become, for better and for worse. It was

In spite of the fact that there have been many exhibitions of his work in Italy and abroad, and although his work has been produced in several richly illustrated catalogue-books, the basic fact that Dario Fo is a painter as well as writer still comes as a surprise to many.[18] His art has yet to receive the focused criticism he deserves, and the brief discussion here is no substitute. Only Emilio Tadini and Fabio Rodriguez Amaya have devoted any serious attention to Fo the artist, and even they in short essays. Dario's work does not hang in any of the great galleries of Italy. Many canvases are leaning against a wall in the attic of his home in Milan, others have been framed by friends who have been recipients of gifts, others are lying in the store rooms of theatres while an inestimable number of drawings are scrawled on the frontispieces of books as dedication to recipients. Rodriguez Amaya imagines the mixture of disbelief and wonder with which some future cataloguer or museum keeper will pull out from various cases:

... at random some of the thousands of sheets of paper and cartoons bristling with polychrome images. There will suddenly
come to life blue minotaurs, cloth puppets, fierce monsters,
damsels in gilded peplums, groups of lovers under dark colon-
nades, ironical putti staring out of windows, metaphysical cita-
dels, elaborate codices, ships raising anchor, prancing horses,
portraits of the eternal muse.[19]

Although some work won prizes and was accepted for exhibitions when
he was young, his first major exhibition, *Teatro nell'occhio* (Theatre in the
Eye) was held in Riccione 1984. With many additions and alterations, this
exhibition was toured to many galleries around the world, to be succeeded by *Pupazzi con Rabbia e Sentimento* (Puppets with Rage and Feeling)
first seen in Cesenatico in 1998. The following year Milan hosted a joint
exhibition of designs by Fo and Fellini, and there were other exhibitions
which featured the drawings he did in preparation for productions of his
plays. In 2010, *Il Centro per l'Arte Otello Cirri* in Pontedera mounted a ret-
rospective exhibition, including puppets, tapestries, working sketches as
well as canvases executed in his youth. Finally in January 2012, the Palazzo Reale in Milan was home to what must be the definitive exhibition,
Lazzi sberleffi dipinti (Stage Routines, Sniggers and Paintings) with over
four hundred works covering the whole range of Fo's output - paintings,
sketches, costumes, masks, puppets, photography as well as filmed foot-
age.

Dario's canvases display a wide diversity of styles and subjects, as is
to be expected of any artist who has been active over a span of 50 years.
Compilers of catalogues and curators of exhibitions divide Fo's work into
various phases: his early "free works," his sketches for particular productions (which were often fully painted works of art),[20] designs for the
productions of Rossini operas, illustrations for his art criticism books,
re-working of classical canvases, portraits of Franca and works inspired
by his love for Greek civilisation. The early work was given a careful fin-
ish, while much of the later work is evidently more hurried. He came
close to many trends and schools, and was influenced at differing times
by many artists without ever throwing in his lot with any one and without
losing his own individuality. From the outset he preferred figurative, not
abstract art,

The earliest canvases of any artist are normally given the heading 'juve-
nilia,' but already at the age of 16, for example in a self-portrait in pencil
and water colour dated 1942, he showed a remarkable sureness of touch.

He says he had already started painting when still at primary school, and the first painting he remembers doing was a copy of a portrait of Cavour. This work caught the attention of his teacher, who encouraged him. There are three self-portraits dating from 1942-49, all showing a serious, un-smiling youth looking out challengingly at the viewer and at the world be-yond. The most introspective is the 1948 oil painting, in which face and shoulders are shown against a light blue background. It would be easy for the professional critic to isolate echoes of Picasso, Gauguin, Chagall or De Kooning, but whether reproducing landscapes around Lake Maggiore, painting female nudes or proving cartoon treatments of scenes from Tol-stoy, the freshness of eye, the clarity of line, the boldness of colour, the impeccable pictorial resolution and fidelity of representation are char-acteristics which shine through. The influences of the painters renowned in his youth, such as the cubism of Léger or Picasso, are evident in such work as the portrait, known as *La dattilografa* (The Typist), a figure seat-ed amidst an assortment of unrelated shapes. At times his strokes are understated, at times they have a strength which causes them to explode in riotous exuberance. There are many treatments of the female nude, as there would be all throughout his life, and while some writers have spoken of these as part of the academic training of young artists, this judgment overlooks the high erotic charge present in the paintings, and discussed in theoretical-historical terms in books written in later life. The body is king, or queen, and this is no aesthetically distant or styl-ised female body, but flesh and blood women, young, alluring and sexy. The female nude is not exactly an unfamiliar figure in western art, but the priapic, sensual, carnival carnality and joyousness of Fo's nudes, both the static portraits painted as a young student at the Brera or rings of Grecian dancing girls drawn for theatre works of later years, are overwhelming. They may be nymphs fleeing the unwanted attention of satyrs, young men and women in uninhibited, improbable gymnastic romps, fantastic fig-ures rolling and gyrating in incomprehensible and unarrestable motion, but there is the sense that some drama, perhaps unseen by the viewer, is being played out. Nothing is more disconcerting than the sheer erotic excess of much of this work. There is no trace of guilt or self-questioning detectable in these pagan, corybantic depictions of sexual exhilaration.

Fo stated many times that he had initially wished to be a painter not a writer, or even that he was an amateur actor and a professional artist. Critics have reversed this assertion. If his theatre has been conditioned by his painterly eye, his artwork, and not only that which began life as

preparatory work for productions, is dramatic in conception and execution. His figures, apart from some posed portraits, are in constant
motion. What is absent is any form of abstract art. Dario expressed his
distaste for any élite or avant-garde in theatre, and the absence of any
such style in painting is silent evidence of the same trend. He was fully
involved in the debates on realism and neo-realism in 1940s Milan, and
used only such elements of cubism as could be reconciled with figurative
art. He was part of that democratic movement, which found expression in
the periodical *Realismo*, which sought to ensure that art maintained a dialogue with the tastes of ordinary people and did not appeal only to a small
circle of aesthetes. At this time, Fo executed some delightful still lifes and
landscapes reminiscent in execution to the work of the Macchiaioli.

There is no point in guessing how Fo might have developed as an artist,
or what level of renown he might have won, but for most of his career, his
artwork was done in conjunction with his work in the theatre. Christopher Cairns underlines one of the more remarkable aspects of this when
he draws attention to Fo's "visual language based on an artistic culture
(which is itself grounded) on the study of the great artists of European
painting."[21] The engagement of Fo with the European tradition, both in
theatre and in art, is one of his most striking characteristics, and Cairns
identifies echoes of Picasso, Goya, Chagall among many others in works
which were executed as the preparatory work of a writer-director-de-
signer. The imaginative exuberance of Fo should not be neglected. While
rehearsing for *Isabella tre caravelle e un cacciaballe* (1963, Isabella, Three
Caravels and a Con-Man) he produced an ink drawing of a crowded trip-
tych with various scenes of a man being hanged, a naked couple kissing,
and Columbus displaying the globe to the queen all packed into a limited
space. His production of *The Barber of Seville* allowed him to release his
imagination on Spanish art, while work for *Il papa e la strega* (1989, The
Pope and the Witch) contained a mural featuring unusually roguish, extremely naked women cavorting in a decorated room in Fo's imaginary
Vatican.

For the final exhibition in the Palazzo Reale, he enlisted the assistance
of students from the Academy to form a *bottega* to help in the execution
of his work. He sketched outlines in pencil and told them which colours
to use. Some of this work was more explicitly political than his previous
art had been. *Lo sbarco di Lampedusa* (Disembarcation at Lampedusa) is
an overtly didactic piece on the tragedy of North Africans trying to reach
Europe and dying while making the crossing, while a canvas alongside

it carried the ironic words, *L'umana accoglienza è sinonimo di democrazia* (A Human Welcome is Synonymous with Democracy). A painting of the bridge over the straits of Messina, a project proposed by Berlusconi, recalls Bosch's *Torri di Babele* (Tower of Babel), while *Una serata tranquilla alla casa del Drago* (A Quiet Evening in the Dragon's Home) has some nude girls dancing bunga-bunga around Berlusconi. If there is some evidence of Christian symbolism, for example in the canvas depicting a kiss between Christ and Mary Magdalene or scenes from the life of St. Francis, Dario was always inspired more strongly by the Greeks or the epics of the late middle ages. *Sequenza degli amori* (Sequence of Loves), inspired by Ovid, gives his sensuality full expression, while the whirlpool of movement and the range of coloured figures in various poses in *Il ratto di Europa* (The Rape of Europa) shows Dario combining his most thoughtful moods with exuberance of imagination.

REFERENCES

1   Interview with Dario Fo, *Il Tirreno*, 17 April 2010.

2   Interview with Dario Fo by Paolo Landi, in *Il teatro dell'occhio*, Firenze, La Casa usher, 1985, p.20.

3   Interview with Dario Fo, *L'Arena*, 28 August 2007.

4   The full text with illustration by Fo was published as *Lezione sul Cenacolo di Leonardo*, San Lazzaro di Savena, Nuovi Mondi, 2001: second edition, revised, Modena, Franco Cosimo Panini, 2007.

5   Emilio Tadini, *Quelle figure da non perdere d'occhio*, in *Il teatro dell'occhio*, cit., p.10

6   Dario Fo, *La vera Storia di Ravenna*, Modena, Franco Cosimo Panini, 1999.

7   Dario Fo, *Il tempio degli uomini liberi: il Duomo di Modena*, Modena, Franco Cosimo Panini, 2004.

8   Henry Adams, *Mont Saint Michel and Chartres*, New York, Mentor Books, 1961, p.25.

9   Dario Fo, *Caravaggio al tempo di Caravaggio*, Modena, Franco Cosimo Panini, 2005, p 30

10   Dario Fo, *Il Mantegna impossibile*, Modena, Franco Cosimo Panini, 2006, p12.

11   Interview in *La Gazzetta di Mantova*, 4 July 2006

12   Dario Fo, *Correggio che dipingeva appeso in cielo*, Modena, Franco Cosimo Panini, 2010.

13   Dario Fo, *Bello Figliolo che Tu Sei Raffaello*, Modena, Franco Cosimo Panini, 2006, p60.

14   Dario Fo, *Tegno nelle Mane Occhi e Orecchi, Michelagniolo*, Modena, Franco Cosimo Panini, 2007.

15   Intervista ne *Il Corriere del Veneto*, 20 February 2005

16   Dario Fo, *Giotto o non Giotto*, Modena, Franco Cosimo Panini, 2010.

17   Dario Fo, edited by Franca Rame and Giselda Palombi, *Sant'Ambrogio e l'invenzione di Milano*, Turin, Einaudi, 2009.

18   The major catalogue-books are: *Il teatro dell'occhio*, cit.:Dario Fo, *Pupazzi con rabbia e sentimento*, Milan, Libri Schweiller, 1998: Federico Fellini e Dario Fo, *Disegni geniali*, Milan, Mazzotta, 1999: Dario Fo e Franca Rame, edited by Luciano Silva, *Una vita per l'arte*,

L'arte per una vita, Milan, Elle Esse, 2002: *Pupazzi con rabbia e sentimento: la vita e l'arte di Dario Fo e Franca Rame*, Edizioni Festival Sete Sòis Sete Luas, 2010: Dario Fo a Milano, *Lazzi sberleffi dipinti*, Milan, Mazzotta, 2012.

19   Fabio Rodriguez Amaya, *Un artista completo: Dario Fo tra impegno, ludus e creatività*, in *Una vita per l'arte, L'arte per una vita*, cit.

20   Christopher Cairns, *Dario Fo e la "pittura scenica": arte teatro regie 1977-1997*, Naples, Edizioni Scientifiche Italiane, 2000.

21   Christoper Cairns, op. cit., p28.

Chapter 4

AN IRREGULAR WARRIOR: CIVILISATION AND THE APOCALYPSE

In an interview in late 1990, Dario stated that his theatre would in future be devoted predominantly to social criticism since he had grown tired of political satire. "The Super-SID (Defence Service Information)? The secret services? Conspiracies? Enough! These things don't tempt us any more. The protagonists of our political life are minor, tiny, mediocre characters."[1] In spite of this vehemence, he was not planning to go home and cultivate his garden. His image of himself as a writer would not permit him to relax into the role of a GOM who was society's darling, or to become Browning's *Lost Leader*, who had sold out for "just a ribbon to stick in his hair." The statement made clear his intention of continuing to adopt a critical and satirical stance, but in a different area of life. Politics in a narrow sense was not the field on which he planned to spend the rest of his life jousting, or so it seemed.

It was, however, an ill-chosen moment to be declaring a loss of interest in politics in Italy since the seemingly immutable political landscape was about to be shaken by a series of earthquakes. Fo's home city of Milan would be the first to experience the tremors, and the first in which the new battles would be fought. The First Republic was falling apart, and the old lords were being removed from their estates while new men strode onto the land. The political parties which had dominated Italian government during the post-war era disintegrated, and new forces emerged, the first of which, the Lombard League, later the Northern League, led by Umberto Bossi, emerged on Dario's own doorstep. He was delighted with the overthrow of the old forces, but found himself as hostile to the new powers as he had been to the old.

It was, and has remained, hard to pin down the exact political objectives and the constitutional aims of the League. At varying times, it has been in favour of the decentralisation of greater power to Lombardy, federalism in Italy and the independence of an imprecisely defined area known as the North. The advocacy of regional decentralisation was reinforced when Bossi became familiar with the events in Scotland which added the word "devolution' to the Italian political lexicon. Bossi himself was very impressed with Mel Gibson's film *Braveheart,* and even had a portrait of himself painted in the outfit worn by William Wallace in the film. The results of the 1997 devolution referendum were released as Bossi was entering Venice after sailing along the Po carrying a cruet he had filled with water at the source of the river and intended to pour ceremonially into the Venetian lagoon. The meaning of this gesture was never quite made clear. The city itself was festooned with posters congratulating the Scots on their choice and inviting the Milanese, Turinese, Venetians and even Florentines (although the latter were a borderline case) to follow their example. Later, the League changed its stance to federalism, with Italy divided into three maxi-regions, and even to complete independence, but there was in its programme an ever-present undercurrent of anti-southern and anti-Sicilian feeling which later became overt racism against third-world immigrants. The fiscal policies advocated by the League intended to tilt the distribution of national resources away from the poorer South in favour of the more prosperous and industrialised north of the country.

Caught as unprepared as the majority of Italians, Dario soon declared himself implacably opposed to the League and, like many left-wingers, found himself in the paradoxical position of giving the Italian state the support he had withheld during the terrorist crisis. During a demonstration on 20 September 1997 in Piazza Duomo in Milan, the scene of the great trade-union and leftist demonstrations in the sixties, he was to be seen on the platform singing, admittedly with ironic comments, the Italian national anthem and waving the tricolour vigorously in the face of League hecklers, an act which drew the approval even of such right-wing journalists as Indro Montanelli, editor of *Il Giornale,* and a long-time opponent of Fo and Rame. However, Bossi, while subjected by Dario and Franca to contemptuous satirical remarks, never received from them the same focused attention accorded to Silvio Berlusconi and his party, *Forza Italia!* After his "entry to the field" in 1994, as Berlusconi described his decision to enter politics, it was he who would become the principal object of Fo's scorn and satire over coming years.

The slow, messy fall of the First Republic and the transition to the Second Republic had multiple causes, one of which was the *Mani Pulite* (Clean Hands) campaign led by a group of magistrates in Milan headed by Antonio di Pietro. In February 1992, Mario Chiesa, an official in the PSI (Italian Socialist Party) and director of the Pio Albergo Trivulzio, a charitable institution founded in the later eighteenth century to provide for the elderly poor, was arrested. Initially it seemed a normal criminal case involving one corrupt individual, and Chiesa was denounced as such by Bettino Craxi, leader of the PSI, a decision Craxi was to rue. Chiesa was in fact collecting bribes payable to the PSI, and when the police arrived to execute a warrant for his arrest, they found him trying to flush away banknotes for millions of lire. Chiesa's detention is commonly taken as the first act in the unfolding scandal which was given the journalistic title, *Tangentopoli*, which can be approximately rendered as Bribesville. Over the coming months and years, it was revealed that Italy had been governed by systemic political-financial corruption, and that those responsible were on the one hand the political parties who had, in various combinations and coalitions, dominated Parliament in recent decades, and on the other the managers and directors of the great Italian corporations. Politicians at all levels – town and city council, provincial, regional and national government – found themselves under investigation, as did previously unsuspected business leaders. Di Pietro became a national hero, and remained a beacon of moral probity, even when his political inadequacy became apparent. Franca Rame in particular was drawn to him, but both Dario and Franca gave him, and other magistrates all over Italy, their full support.

The sense of national outrage was almost palpable as Italians, who had never held politicians in high regard, turned on those who had misgoverned the country. One by one the previous governing parties dissolved, disintegrated or disappeared. The Christian Democrats, who had been in every government in Rome since the end of World War II, splintered into many segments. The Socialists too broke apart and Craxi fled to Tunisia to escape arrest, and died there. The Social Democrats simply vanished and even older parties like the Republicans and the Liberals who could trace their origins back to the Risorgimento were swept aside. The Communist party was not immune to this process of national cleansing once it was shown that some of the previously admired co-operatives in their stronghold of Emilia-Romagna had indulged in corrupt practices. However in their case the essential cause of their demise was the fall of the Berlin Wall, the collapse of the Soviet Unity and a vague but irresistible sense that the Marxist dream as it had been incarnated until that point in history was no longer tenable. In November 1999, the then Communist leader, Achille Occhetto, announced in Bologna that change was inevitable. Although the main component continued as the Democrats of the Left, other factions split off. The party was a busted flush.

Fo's support for the *Clean Hands* campaign was reflected in a new play *Settimo ruba un po' meno, No.2* (Seventh Commandment: Steal a little Less, No.2), first staged in November 1992. The work, as the No.2 in the title suggested, was the recycling of a comedy staged twenty-five years earlier when the attack on corruption was recounted in a series of scenes which seemed then as fantastic as episodes in *Gulliver's Travels*. The core incidents in the earlier play were "absurd events dealing with speculation on bodies waiting to be buried at the Musocco cemetery," Dario explained, but what seemed wildly surreal yesterday was the subject of daily press reports as the misdeeds of politicians in every party came to light. "We have made the discovery that our script has been plundered, obviously without us receiving a lira from the SIAE (Italian Society of Authors and Editors)," complained Dario. The new piece was performed by Franca alone, standing at a lectern but improvising freely, moving about on the stage against a backcloth of the faces of the politicians and industrialists, national and local, whose names had surfaced in the investigations. There were several banners on display, one of which read — "Let the Right be ignorant of what the Left is stealing." The script had the violence and scatological force which Dario had detected in his readings of Ruzante and the jesters. When the scene of Chiesa attempting to flush millions of lire down the toilet was acted on stage, the flush mechanism failed to work and the toilet overflowed, leaving Chiesa uncomfortably and embarrassingly drenched in faeces. Another scene shows Di Pietro having one of the accused injected with some substance to make him stop talking, since he fears the courts will be unable to cope with the sheer number of prosecutions made necessary by the volume of revelations. Another incident incorporated into the script concerned the use of a frozen ball, a device seemingly used by the health authorities to ensure that the "correct" person was chosen as consultant at one of the most prestigious hospitals in Milan. Officially the choice was made by drawing lots: ten balls were put in a bag, each with a name written on it, and the one selected at random got the job. To make sure there were no "mistakes", the ball with the name of the person who had paid the highest bribe was put into a refrigerator one hour previously, and so could be instantly identified.

The principal aim and justification of satire, as Fo has repeated continually throughout his career, is the revelation of the strutting absurdity of authority in an attempt to cause the hierarchy of established power to tot-ter. The methods may be savage, as were the proposals advanced by Jona-than Swift in his *Modest Proposal*, a work Fo admires, and such savagery is justified provided it is not gratuitous. Satire of its nature, he believes, in-volves the exposure of authority figures to ridicule, showing them in their underpants, caricaturing their tricks of speech or habits of mind, por-traying them as slobbering drunkards when they have advocated sobriety. They are metaphorically put in the stocks and the missiles of laughter are launched at them. Satire employs the grotesque, another recurrent word in the Fo vocabulary, and is offensive by nature. On this occasion, cari-cature was hardly necessary, and Bettino Craxi in particular emerged not as a dignified statesman, but as a smirking buffoon. The revived *Seventh Commandment* is a work of bitter indignation spiced with comic force, and may well be one of the most successful works produced by the Fo-Rame couple in this style. It staged and illustrated contemporary circum-stances and focused on issues of the time. If it will not enter the catalogue of works likely to outlast the authors, the jeering tone chimed in with the public mood. There was nothing gratuitous about mockery of the politi-cians or officials here, any more than there was in the classical works in this genre, those of Juvenal, Jonathan Swift or William Hogarth.

Dario brought greater indignation and gravitas to bear on the new de-velopments in the tormented case in which he had been personally, po-litically and morally involved since 1969, and which had been the basis of *Accidental Death of an Anarchist*. The story unfolded over the decades, with different participants in the tragedy taking on the central role in turn. Much has been written from all angles on the linked cases of Pino Pinelli, Luigi Calabresi and Adriano Sofri, so only the merest summary is offered here, and discussion is limited to the involvement of Fo and Rame. The first event was the bombing of the bank at Piazza Fontana in Milan which left 17 people dead and almost 90 injured. Blame was laid, with suspi-cious speed, at the door of some anarchist groups, and Pietro Valpreda in Rome and Pino Pinelli in Milan were arrested. It was later established beyond all doubt that the two men were completely innocent and that the outrage was the work of neo-Fascist elements. Immediately after the ex-plosion, Pinelli was picked up in an anarchist club in the Navigli district of Milan and invited to come to the police station for questioning, which he did on his own scooter. He never emerged alive. His body ended up on the courtyard of the police HQ, where some journalists were gathered waiting for developments. Had he committed suicide? Had he been killed in police custody, perhaps unintentionally as a result of brutal interrogation techniques? Had his body been thrown from the window, or had he jumped? In the aftermath of Pinelli's death, many journalists and activists on the left held commissario Luigi Calabresi responsible for the anarchist's mysterious death, although this was always denied. He was in fact charged with murder, but the prosecutor decided not to proceed with the case. The far left group, *Lotta continua*, who published a periodical of the same name edited by Adriano Sofri, ran a campaign against him which can be viewed as defamatory in the extreme or as a courageous episode in investigative journalism, but it squarely claimed Calabresi was responsible for Pinelli's death. Calabresi took the journal to court for publishing such allegations, but he himself was assassinated on 17 May 1972 while the trial was underway. At the time, no one was arrested for the crime, and the murder became embroiled in conspiracy theories, one of the more persistent in leftist circles being that he was killed by the secret services who were worried about his mental instability as the trial ran on, and were concerned about what he might reveal.

In subsequent years, assessments of Calabresi the man and his motives have varied enormously, so that he now seems a Pirandellian character, elusive and unknowable in himself and with different personalities imposed on him by others. Two Popes have referred to him as a man of faith, almost a martyr, and the process of beatification was initiated under Pope John Paul II. His widow published a moving book on his personal qualities,[2] while the director Marco Tullio Giordana gave a very positive portrait of him in his 2011 film, *Romanzo di una strage* (Novel of a Massacre). His son is now editor of the Turin-based newspaper, *La Stampa*, and has always, unsurprisingly, proclaimed his father's innocence. Others have continued to portray Calabresi has as a torturer and even as a murderer. More recently, Dario Fo has declared that he viewed Calabresi as one of the victims of one of the more sinister mysteries of twentieth-century Italian political life.

In *Accidental Death*, he appears as the "sporting" commissario dressed in the roll-top jumper which Calabresi was frequently pictured wearing. Fo's portrayal of him in the play is hostile, although without any allegations of guilt for murder. The 1974 edition of the play has a postface signed by *La Comune*, the co-operative in which Fo was then working and which first staged the play in 1990, saying that the trial of the case for defamation brought by Calabresi was "suspended on account of *force majeure* (the non accidental death of the actor)."[3] This remark is callous at the very least, but it part of was a joint statement, not written by Fo in person.

Although there is an obvious continuity between them, it is useful to divide the sorry saga into three episodes: the Pinelli case itself, the Calabresi case and the Sofri-Bompressi-Pietrostafani case. This last act unfolded in the years from 1988 onwards, and it was this which brought Fo and Rame back into the case, particularly since they knew Adriano Sofri. In 1988 Sofri, together with Ovidio Bompressi and Giorgio Pietrostefani, two other ex-members of Lotta continua, were arrested and charged with the murder of Calabresi. The news of the arrests caused consternation, not least because Sofri, like many other Sixties revolutionaries, had in the intervening years become a familiar, well-connected figure in the best salons of Milan and Rome, as well as writer and journalist. The case became a *cause célèbre*, and was taken up by writers and intellectuals including Vincenzo Consolo, Umberto Eco, Dacia Maraini, Carlo Ginzburg, all of whom were convinced of his innocence. Dario made reference to the arrests in his Nobel Prize speech, calling them "a justice farce, an insult to reason."

It transpired that the *carabinieri* who made the arrest relied on the testimony of one informer, Leonardo Marino, who had also been in *Lotta Continua* in the '70s. Marino claimed to have been the driver of the car used for the killing, although contemporary eye-witnesses all agreed that the person at the steering wheel was a woman. As a result of Marino's allegations, Bompressi was accused of being the actual killer and Sofri and Pietrostefani of having masterminded the operation. According to police accounts Marino made his confession on 20 July 1988, but it emerged that he had been in the police station since 2 July. The accounts given by Marino in the course of the various trials were contradictory on many details, and differed from the accounts provided by eye-witnesses. There were many glaring inconsistencies. He suggested, for instance, that he had been overwhelmed by an onrush of guilt, especially after a conversation with a Salesian priest. In the witness box, the priest denied having ever set eyes on him.

The judicial history of the Sofri-Bompressi-Pietrostefani case has been a disgrace to Italian justice, and was subjected to masterly dissection by the historian Carlo Ginzburg, who saw parallels with sixteenth-century witch trials.[4] In all, there were 7 trials in 9 years with different outcomes, but at the conclusion of this process all three men were given lengthy prison sentences. Some of Sofri's supporters appealed to the President for a pardon, but Sofri himself refused to associate himself with this appeal since he viewed it as incompatible with his insistence on his innocence. Dario and Franca backed the campaign for Sofri's release, and in 1998 when the legal process seemed to be finally exhausted - in fact there were several more rounds to come - Dario wrote *Marino libero! Marino innocente!* (Marino Free! Marino Innocent!),[5] a work which drew heavily on the writings of Ginzburg as well as on his own knowledge and research. The lecture-cum-performance was illustrated by slides and diagrams, reproduced in the published version. He subjected the hapless Marino, and the judges, to a barrage of ridicule, anger and scorn, all based on rational argument of a force worthy of Voltaire on the Calas affair.

Marino presented himself as a *pentito* (literally a repentant terrorist) who merited the special treatment Italian law afforded such people. He claimed to be devoured by guilt for his past crimes, but the judges considered him one of the guilty men and imposed a prison sentence on him too. Fo's title is an ironic defence of Marino's innocence and a sardonic advocacy of his claim for immediate release, accomplished by showing Marino to be a liar, and therefore his evidence on the three main accused unreliable. The man himself was represented by a little puppet which sat on Dario's knee, and which, according to the stage directions, "will be animated, interrogated, caressed an even slapped" in mock encouragement or irritation during the performance. The purpose of the monologue, Dario tells his spectators, is "to recount to you the follies, the absurdities, the lies invented by Marino, by the judges and the carabineri." His mathematics were precise. The total number of "lies, absurd declarations or egregious errors came to 120." The work combines forensic skill with expressions of outrage, interspersed with episodes of pantomime clowning, although at times there was no need of creative farce, since the words of Marino and the judges were beyond satire. One judicial statement, reported literally by Fo, stated that "Marino was educated by the Salesian Fathers and it is known that anyone who comes from a Salesian background never lies." Fo established, with detailed reference to sketches of his own and street plans of the district where the crime was committed, the inconsistency and mendacity of Marino's evidence, even if he had studied with the Salesians.

The work was broadcast on Radio Popolare, and was transmitted on RAI2 on 17 March 1998. The broadcasts aroused public protests, but alas! literature and drama, as poets and playwrights have discovered from the days of the Spanish Civil War, have limited use as instruments of politics. Sofri remained in prison, and was released only in 2012 on the expiry of his sentence.

Dario and Franca took part in events commemorating the victims of the 'years of lead'. In December 1999, on the thirtieth anniversary of the bombing in Piazza Fontana, they participated in the Caravan of Truth and Memory, which saw them hire a train which went from Brescia, where there was a ceremony of remembrance for the eight people killed by a neo-Fascist group in 1974 while taking part in a trade union demonstration, to Milan for a march proceeded by a band which escorted them to Piazza Fontana. The following day, the train proceeded to Bologna, Florence and Rome, cities which had seen terrorist outrages. At each stop, they unfurled drapes designed by Dario with the help of students in Art Schools around Italy. In Rome a delegation, including Dario and Franca, was received in the Quirinal Palace by President Carlo Azeglio Ciampi. However, not all those who had been activists in those days wished to remember their part, and Franca wrote of her dismay on seeing "comrades" from the days of militant campaigns appear on television as lawyers or PR representatives for multinational corporations. The Sofri case made them wonder whether much had changed. Power resided where it always had, and behaved as it always had.

Dario considered writing a play about the violence perpetrated by the police against protesters during the G8 summit in Genova in 2001, and he continued to call for an investigation into the death of Carlo Giuliani and the conduct of the police during their raid on the Diaz school where protesters were sleeping. However, his main energies were now directed elsewhere, towards the ethics of scientific research and to environmental issues, as he had already indicated during the Nobel Prize ceremonies in Stockholm. In a televised debate with the other Nobel laureates, he attacked those scientists guilty of amoral cynicism in their indifference to the ends which their research served. He branded them "people for whom there is no difference between a plutonium bomb and a machine for cleansing the polluted deposits in the sea." He was unhappy with the statement of an American Nobel who complained against US government cuts in funding for military research, believing that this would have a detrimental knock-on effect on all scientific research. Fo found himself on the same side as the Pope, whose "proclamations against war and against murderous experimentation on human beings are sacrosanct."[6] Fo and Pope John Paul II, although they never met, tended to see eye to eye on many issues.

Over the following years, he invited controversy by venturing into green politics, and expressing opinions on such disparate subjects as global warming, bio-engineering, GM crops and other problems created by modern science, medicine and technology. Current trends in scientific research dismayed him, and the prospect of human cloning in particular shocked him. In the Nobel Prize speech, he voiced his horror on hearing of an American researcher who was attempting to produce a humanoid clone without a brain for use as a source of spare parts in transplant surgery. He gave speeches, appeared before committees, wrote books and did lecture-performances on his fears for a future dominated by big industry and backed by scientists devoid of humanist philosophy and unchecked by ethical considerations. News of the cloning of Dolly the sheep in a laboratory in Edinburgh, the city where the tale of Dr Jekyll and Mr Hyde was conceived, horrified him.

In February 1998, he accepted an invitation from a specialist committee of the European Parliament in Strasbourg to give evidence, which he then published in a pamphlet entitled *"To Oppose the Copyright of Genes, There is no Need to be a Genus* (sic)." His specific objection was to a directive approved by the Parliament which allowed the copyrighting of human organs. "I called it the Frankenstein pig brother operation," he declared shortly afterwards. What began life as a scientific paper, even if one not couched in conventional academic jargon, became a performance piece, *L'uomo porco e il porco uomo* (The pig-man and the man-pig), performed in Lugano in May.[7] The title referred to the fact that some medical researchers had attempted to implant embryos into pigs in the hope that they would provide organs that could be used in human transplants. The script included a grotesque twist typical of Fo. A sow has ovaries implanted in her womb, and begins to show pre-humanoid tendencies, including the ability to say "Mamma and Papa." Dario had a photo-montage made of him with pig's trotters instead of feet. "Beware the pork-man" was the satirical slogan coined to protest against developments in bio-engineering.

With no background in science, he was aware he was on thin ice and risked being made to appear an opponent of research, so he always went out of his way to add the proviso that he was not a luddite opponent of scientific advance but only of the unethical misuse and application of scientific discoveries. He delivered a widely reported speech at a conference, *Ten Nobel Prize-Winners for the Future*, which included among its participants Rita Levi Montalcini, the Italian scientist awarded the Nobel Prize in 1986 for her work in neurobiology but who claimed not to have heard of Fo when the announcement of Nobel Prize to him was made. Later the two became friends and Levi Montalcini would be one of Franca's few allies in the Italian senate. Fo's speech was a sally against genetic manipulation, in which he invoked Leonardo da Vinci, who had written in his notebooks that there were certain findings he would not publish for fear of the damage they might cause. One scientist wrote to the *Corriere della Sera* asking if Dario believed that anyone who received an international award has the automatic right to deliver opinions on all topics, and asking him not to misuse his gifts as entertainer and satirist to stir up public opinion against research in delicate areas.[8] Dario replied that he had the same right to attack genetic engineering as he had had to attack nuclear technology, and that his concerns were shared by scientists.

Over the coming decade, he became increasingly outspoken on global warming, pollution, the over-exploitation of the planet's resources and the future prospects for humanity on a planet where human life had been made unsustainable by the human destruction of the ecology. Fo was viewed in some quarters as a trespasser in areas of which he had no knowledge, in others as a prophet of doom, but making use of his familiar weapons - humour, irony, wit and a feeling for the absurd - he set himself on a mission to warn humanity of the fate that many environmentalists feared lay ahead. *L'apocalisse rimandata, ovvero Benvenuta catastrophe!* (The Apocalypse Postponed or Welcome Catastrophe!), a work which he performed around Italy before publishing it in book form in 2008, exemplifies his approach.[9] The cover illustration shows a grotesque Moloch with several mouths, each one devouring a baby. The saving cataclysm for humanity arrives when the oil reserves are exhausted and cars, buses and trains can no longer run. A blackout affects the world's great population centres and modern mass media cease to function. Civilisation does not collapse into the war of all against all, as Thomas Hobbes in *Leviathan* believed was the natural condition of pre-political humankind, but instead human beings alter their way of living and, significantly, rediscover older values and ways of life rather than devise new ones. Not all the established authorities are equal to the challenge. The Pope, for instance, fails to capitalise on the opportunity the crisis offers for implementing the beliefs of St Francis of Assisi, whose teachings were of growing interest to Dario, as was the notion that small could be beautiful. This truth had been demonstrated, he came to believe, by the cultural and political practices of the medieval city-states of northern and central Italy. The culture and civilization on which the political order is founded require to be reformed to make them based not on competition and repression, the core canons of capitalism, but on spontaneous, willing cooperation between human beings and on a quest for harmony with nature.

In one sense these ideas are a logical development of the socialist ideology to which he had always adhered, but they also represent a move to a new dimension, to a focus, however whimsically expressed, on the ideological underpinnings of the political. He adapted for green ends Gramsci's teaching that culture supported the hegemonic political structure, and that there was an ignored, popular culture which could be employed for reform. The coming environmental cataclysm, if steps are not taken to head it off, could lead to the construction of a new, fairer society. It is, as he wrote, an apocalyptic scenario.

Increasing frustration with contemporary politicians led Dario to consider entering politics by himself. His concern over green issues was one impulse, and in autumn 2000, he and Franca began advocating the use of rape-seed oil instead of petrol as fuel on public transport. He gave grudging support to a campaign in Milan to have twelve car-free Sundays a year, but believed the measure inadequate in itself. "The truth is that they (i.e. such token measures) touch interests which are too great, starting with Seven Sisters of the oil industry. There needs to be greater information."[10] Later that month, both were among the promoters of an anti-pollution, "Clean Air" referendum, which they hoped would be held in May 2001. Dario let it be known that he was contemplating standing for mayor of Milan. His hope was to be adopted as candidate of the Centre-Left alliance but his candidature caused splits and dissension, and he oscillated for a time before declaring in January that he would withdraw, saying, "I am not a bumpy wheel, nor a Don Quixote sent into the fray by someone who then poisons his steed," he said, enigmatically. He also feared his candidature would threaten the precarious unity of the Left. Franca, however, was given the position as leading figure in the list of candidates for the group *Miracolo a Milano*. She was not elected. The new mayor was Gabriele Albertini, a member of Berlusconi's Pole of Freedoms coalition of parties.

The main points of the proposed 2001 electoral programme – traffic, corruption, pollution, bureaucracy, urban planning and city cleansing – re-appeared on his programme when he presented himself, this time unequivocally, as candidate for Mayor in 2006. The decision to stand was motivated by his customary mixture of indignation and enthusiasm, indignation over the condition of Milan and over the confusion inside the

Left, enthusiasm for the task of introducing anti-pollution and reform measures to improve conditions of life in the city. The Left was grouped in a broad, disputatious coalition called simply the Union, and the candidate was to be chosen by the democratic system of primaries. Dario rejected the widespread belief that only "a moderate" would make an acceptable candidate, viewing this belief as a symptom of a loss of confidence among left-wingers. He wished to propose radical measures to confront the problems of the city and of Italian society. "I am no moderate", declared a poem printed on the front of his manifesto.

Il moderato è forte con i deboli e debole con i forti
Il moderato finge di risolvere i problemi senza affrontarli
Il moderato chiude un occhio sulle speculazioni edilizie
Il moderato caccia gli inquilini dalle case in centro
E poi li rivende ai magnati della speculazione...

The moderate is strong with the weak and weak with the strong
The moderate pretends to resolve problems without facing them
The moderate turns a blind eye on building scandals
The moderate chases tenants from homes in the centre
And then resells them to the magnates in the scandals ...

Fo received the immediate support of the Greens and of Communist Refoundation, the left-wing splinter group which set up on its own after the disbanding of the old Italian Communist Party. He was inspired by the example of the Labour Mayor of London, Ken Livingstone, "Red Ken", whom he met in December 2005 when he and Franca went to London to attend a rally against the Iraq War. The rally was poorly organised, and Dario's name was inserted among the speakers only at the last minute. Although he had come specially for the event, he was given an unannounced and unpublicized slot during the lunch break when many of the delegates were absent. His speech was interrupted by one of the organisers, a strange little English woman who stood in front of the podium, smiling inanely and making chopping motions with one hand to indicate that Dario should cut his contribution to a maximum of a few minutes. However, if he drew few listeners at that moment, he held the audience in the evening when a monologue of his, *Mamma Pace* (Peace Mum), was performed by the celebrated English actress, Frances De La Tour. This brief work was based on a letter written by the American anti-war activist, Cindy Sheehan, to President George W. Bush. Sheehan's son had been killed in Iraq, and she had gone to camp outside Bush's home in Texas demanding the opportunity to speak to him in person. Her request was refused, but she travelled to London to attend the demonstration, and she and Dario met there. Later that month, Franca performed the piece at a demonstration in Turin of activists in the No TAV movement (No to the High Speed Train), a group opposed to the construction of a high-speed railway line along the Susa valley towards Turin and Lyons. One of the participants at the Turin rally was Beppe Grillo, a comedian who was emerging as leading figure in all anti-government protest movements.

While in London, Dario met Livingstone, and was impressed by the fact the mayor travelled to the hotel where the two were to meet by subway, not in the mayor's official car, which he had sold. "A mayor must use public schools, public transport and public hospitals," Livingstone told him. Dario was particularly interested in the congestion charge Livingstone had introduced as a means of reducing traffic pollution. He was also moved by the fact that Livingstone and other campaigners had used the English title of Dario's play *Can't Pay? Won't Pay!* as a slogan against the hated poll tax introduced years before by Mrs Thatcher. He also had seen all of Dario's plays in translation. It was a partnership made in heaven, and Livingstone accepted an invitation to go to Milan to support Dario's candidacy.

That campaign was addressed, as he put it, to people who wanted to hear the story suppressed by the media in the age of Berlusconi, and was conducted in a mixture of conventional and totally idiosyncratic campaigning methods. He hired a bus which on one occasion went to Piazza della Scala where groups of refugees from Eritrea were protesting in the cold of winter against the failure of the Council to give them shelter. There was a debate underway in the Council Chambers on this question, and some councillors alleged that shelter had been offered but refused by the asylum-seekers, who preferred to pose for the TV camera. "Bugiardo, Vergogna - Liar, Shame" shouted Fo from the public gallery. He told a correspondent from *The Times* who had accompanied him that Milan needed a revolution. When asked if writers should enter politics, he justified his action by pointing to Machiavelli and Leonardo, who had both held political office, as had actors and dramatists in ancient Athens.[11]

His manifesto was detailed, specific and well researched, not limited to general statements of principle, and set out in a brightly coloured pamphlet, illustrated with drawings and sketches by Dario himself. His attacks on the sitting mayor, Gabriele Albertini, were pitiless, while he derided Berlusconi from whom he had received "the most beneficial of lessons. From him I learned what tax havens in holiday islands are, and where real capital, earned in strange and dark ways, can be transferred into fantasy banks ..." The central concerns of his programme was with gas emissions, pollution, energy and housing. He advanced a range of policies, such as one based on the experiences of London and Helsinki, for establishing car parks on the outskirts of Milan to encourage people to travel inside the city by public transport. He attacked planning catastrophes in three areas of the city – Piazzale Dateo, Garibaldi-Repubblica and the ex-Fiera Campionaria, and promised new housing policies, arrived at after discussion with the inhabitants themselves.

Ken Livingstone came for the main rally, held in the Mazdapalace on 21 January, an event which left him stunned. It attracted some 7,000 spectators and was a unique mixture of rally, rock concert, clown show, party, dance exhibition and musical, with political speeches by Ken Livingstone and Fausto Bertinotti, leader of Communist Refoundation, songs by Enzo Jannacci, and a lecture-cum- performance given the title *Sapessi come è strano riuscire ad amarsi a Milano* (If only You Knew How Strange it is to Love Each Other in Milan) written and delivered by Dario. It was all to no avail. The primaries took place a week later and Dario's rival, the ex-prefect Bruno Ferrante, won with 67.6% of the vote against Dario's 23.3%. Dario gave Ferrante his full support in the campaign itself, but in the event he lost to Berlusconi's candidate, Letizia Moratti.

Meantime, Dario had been growing closer to the anti-politics of Beppe Grillo. These two were clearly pre-destined to be soul-mates, both as satirical performers and as political activists. Fo paid Grillo the highest compliment in his vocabulary by calling him a *giullare*, the term he used of himself. While there are important differences, both have a cast of mind which makes them constitutionally ill at ease with the prevailing power structures of society. Both are by temperament as well as belief moved by the sight of injustice, indignant at the abuse of power, frequently hostile to all authority and given to displays of outraged polemics as well as of sardonic, focused, ironic humour. The alliance with Grillo revealed the central traits of Dario's enduring mindset. Rather than a genuine Marxist, he was a permanent outsider or dissident, like St Francis or Vladimir Mayakovsky, a book of whose writings he once edited.[12] He is best described as a utopian anarchist, incapable of accepting the discipline of any political organisation and most at home with ill-regulated groupings, like those that flourished after May 1968. Perhaps Grillo would have remained in the same category had he lived in a pre-Internet age, or had be not encountered Gianroberto Casaleggio, whose views of the potential of the internet and the computer are messianic. Grillo appeared with increasing frequency alongside Dario and Franca at demonstrations or in shows, for example at Forlì in 2009, to oppose plans to destroy part of the countryside in the hope of increasing energy production. His attacks on corruption in public life grew more and more strident and on 8 September 2007, Grillo organised a demonstration known uncompromisingly as the *Vaffa Day*, an assault on the current generation of Italian politicians, expressed in a word Italian mothers found difficult to explain to their offspring. Vaffa is an abbreviation of the semi-obscene but common yell — *vaffanculo*, stick it up your arse. On *Vaffa Day* that invitation was issued to Italy's politicians. Grillo became the focal point and spokesman for growing disgust with politicians and the politics Italian-style, especially among the young.

Having grown exasperated with the limitations of protest movements, in 2009 Grillo founded the *MoVimento 5 Stelle*, the 5 Star Movement, where the five stars have nothing to do with excellence ratings but stand for the central issues on which the party intended to campaign — Water, Environment, Transport, Connectivity and Development. Baffled pundits found the term anti-politics a convenient description for the new body, although it was an inadequate tag for a group whose rise in popularity was registered by a succession of opinion polls. It put up candidates in regional elections, gaining considerable success in Sicily. It was ready to launch itself in the 2013 General Election. Dario gave speeches at several meetings, notably in Milan's Piazza Duomo.

Dario too was in a state of deep exasperation, as was clear from a wide-ranging interview he gave to Euronews earlier that year.[13] In spite of the hopes for renewal he had entertained after the Clean Hands campaign, he declared that Italian politics were once again degraded, but he felt it necessary to look beyond the political dimension in a narrow sense. "If there isn't a system which is strong, solid, and based primarily on culture and knowledge, which instills equality, freedom and justice in the collective consciousness, then everything collapses." Not surprisingly, he identified Berlusconi as the principal source of his country's ills, and still mocked and satirised him:

Just yesterday I did a satirical performance drawn from Buster Keaton. It was about a statue in a large room, and all around there are characters who are trying to keep it up. They move in all directions, they go out, they come back in, they try to support it with mechanical devices to keep it balanced. But the statue falls and is on the verge of breaking. They stand it back up and it's OK again. It comes back, but each time it's closer to the abyss.

The fault with the condition of contemporary society lay with "the banks mostly, and the big entrepreneurs. All those who hold the reins 'the show within a show,' those who – through the media, television and in other ways – make every effort to ensure that the people accept the conditions they find themselves in." He repeated to his interviewer the inadequacy of moderation he had voiced in his mayoral campaign a couple of years previously. Moderates may well wear "the mask of a good person," but it is "really a trap. They appear nice and gentle in their mannerisms and gestures; they never let go, they never have fun, they never play, or dance." They stay in a corner and decline to come forward, he said, summing up his views. This was not his way, especially now that Grillo and his movement seemed to offer a vehicle for change.

His major contribution to the movement in 2013 was his collaboration with Grillo and Casaleggio on a book which had the form of a Platonic dialogue. The three are engaged on an imaginary journey across Greece towards Athens, home of Periclean or direct democracy. The title *Il grillo canta sempre al tramonto: dialogo sull'Italia e il movimento 5 Stelle* (The Cricket Always Sings at Dusk: Dialogue on Italy and the 5 Star Movement) is based on a rather heavy pun on the name of Grillo, a word which in Italian means "cricket."[14] The discussion is in the tradition of European utopian or millenarian literature, in line with works by Thomas More or Tommaso Campanella, but firmly rooted in the age of the computer and internet. "The 5 Star Movement exists thanks to the net," declares Grillo. Fo is not of the Wifi generation, but he saw that if the MoVimento's aims were realised "the whole system is up in the air ... from being a representative democracy the Italian state will become a direct democracy." Casaleggio is the guru of the computer age, and his ideas on the revolutionary potential of the net intrigued many, including American electioneering agents who had no sympathy with his ideology. "The destruction of the planet is at a good point," he said, which meant that "it is necessary to find alternatives to this model of civilisation". All three agree that the apocalypse could not be postponed indefinitely since resources, not only oil, are near to exhaustion. The problems they wish to face are not only corruption and the inequities of late capitalism but also others which are deeper and wider, including "the law which is not applied, workers who die, work itself as blackmail and the reduction of people into slavery." In Casaleggio's analysis, all these problems "at the end of the day come back to the question of money which has taken over all other aspects of life." His solution was that "no-one should possess more than ... 3 or 4 million euros," but interestingly he went on to underline that this was "not a Franciscan but a political point." References to St Francis recur throughout the dialogue, and it was a bit of bad luck for Casaleggio that he complained that there had never been a Pope called Francis only a couple of months before the election to the Papacy of the Argentinian Cardinal Bergoglio, who took the name ... Francis.

The collaboration and cooperative discussion between the three men cannot conceal differences between Dario on the one side and Grillo and Casaleggio on the other. All three are united in disgust with the present system and with the parties and personalities who hold power in it, and all are motivated by open-hearted optimism and idealism. The split, handled amiably, concerns the means to be adopted and the potential of the computer and the internet. For Grillo and Casaleggio, the new technology of the digital age promises wholly new opportunities which could, Casaleggio believes, help individuals even in unlikely areas such as personal health problems. More fundamentally, for the twin seers the computer age could also enable the formation of new non-parties where leaders are dispensable and people can be consulted on all questions. This would make for the creation of the new community, the new governing system and the new culture and civilisation all three believed necessary for the survival of the human race. In Casaleggio's vision, the computer is the equivalent of the philosopher's stone for the alchemists of other times, capable of transforming the base material of traditional political rule into the rosy future of which millenarians had dreamed. Unsurprisingly Dario, while intrigued, remained sceptical about matters in which he was unversed, and suggested to the other two that while they enthused about a virtual online community and its implications for a new democracy, they should not neglect the value of face-to-face communities. He was also dubious when they informed him that he would shortly not be able to rely on expertise of the sort he found in bookshops, since "in a short time, the bookshops to which you are accustomed will no longer be. They will change and may well disappear altogether."

While they drew their inspiration from the new technology and its value in the future, he turned, as he had always done, to history. His interventions contained stories of Charlemagne and of St Francis, as well as discussions of Jacques Le Goff's theories of the invention of Purgatory, of the force of the Italian city-states, or how a group of "irregular warriors" had resisted Federico Barbarossa. An irregular warrior seems an ideal description for Dario himself in politics. In April, during the parliamentary debates over the choice of the new President of the Republic, Grillo proposed him for the office. He declined the offer, so it will never be known how history would have developed had Pope Francis and President Fo been in power at the same time.

REFERENCES

1   *La Repubblica*, 9 November 1990.

2   Gemma Capra, *Mio marito il commissario Calabresi*, Rome, Edizioni Paoline, 1990.

3   Dario Fo, *Morte accidentale di un anarchico*, Turin, Einanudi, 1974, p.111.

4   Carlo Ginzburg, *Il giudice e lo storico*, Turin, Einaudi, 1991

5   Dario Fo, *Marino libero! Marino innocente!*, Turin, Einaudi, 1998.

6   *La Repubblica*, 13 December 1997.

7   *Il Corriere del Ticino*, 27 May 1998.

8   *Il Corriere della Sera*, 15 December 1998.

9   Dario Fo, *L'apocalisse rimandata*, Parma, Guanda, 2008.

10 *Il Corriere della Sera*, 10 June 2000.

11 *The Times*, 24 January 2006.

12 Vladimir Majakovskij, *Messaggi ai posteri selezionati e condivisi da Dario Fo*, Rome, Editori Riuniti, 1994.

13 Interview, 21 February 2013, *What Took Centuries to create in Italy was Degraded in a Very Short Time*. Euronews website, Retrieved January 2015.

14 Dario Fo, Gianroberto Casaleggio, Beppe Grillo, *Il grillo canta sempre al tramonto: dialogo sull'Italia e il movimento 5 Stelle*, Milan, Chiarelettere, 2013.

Chapter 5

FRANCIS AND BERLUSCONI: NON IDENTICAL TWINS

St. Francis of Assisi and Silvio Berlusconi make strange and unexpected bedfellows, but at the turn of the century these two figures and the values they represent stand out, like the church spire and the municipal tower in an Italian medieval hill town, as the most prominent, symbolic presences in the mind, imagination, conscience and therefore theatre of Dario Fo. They made up a perfect Manichean pairing, good and evil, the devil and the angel, the aspirational ideal and the pernicious reality. In moral and political terms, Francis is a reproach to the supposedly Catholic Berlusconi, while in terms of literary technique the idealisation of Francis is the reverse side of the satirical caricature of Berlusconi. References to them arise in unlikely places. The cataclysm imagined in *L'apocalisse rimandata* (2008) gives the reigning Pope the opportunity to preach a return to the purity of the beliefs of St Francis, but he fails to take it. In his pamphlet introducing the DVD of *Ubu Roi – Ubu Bas*, based loosely on the original by Alfred Jarry, Fo reports that when replying to French journalists on restrictions on liberty of expression in Italy, Berlusconi had "said his persecutors were nothing but a gang of *provocateurs*, and defined them as clowns and buffoons." Such a remark was an obvious provocation to Fo, who added his own comment:

> Who are the clowns and the buffoons? Let us be clear that clowns, buffoons and jesters are all part of the same group. St. Francis, talking about himself and his free-wheeling tirades, used to say, "I'm a jester in the service of God!" I don't believe that Francis, defining himself in that way, intended to insult himself![1]

Even in the manifesto-book on the MoVimento, Francis and the Franciscan ethic were summoned by all three authors as ideals and as a corrective to prevailing moral standards in politics and society. Grillo even says he chose St Francis's feast day as the symbolic date for the foundation of his political non-party.

Fo's main works on these two figures are *Lu santo jullàre Francesco* (The Holy Jester Francis) on the one hand and *L'anomalo bicefalo* (The Twin-Headed Anomaly) on the other.[2] His detestation of Berlusconi and his politics is hardly a surprise, but the cult of St Francis requires more consideration. The secular image of Francis has been reshaped for every generation: as a representative of social virtues, as a man imbued with democratic attributes, as a defender of the dispossessed, as an early ecologist, as a lover of animals and nature, as a distruster of hierarchy, as an opponent of power, including ecclesiastical power, and above all a preacher of love and gentleness, perhaps even a pacifist. Arnold Toynbee, in the closing section of his monumental *A Study of History,* defined him as the greatest man in the West, and admired his ideal of the harmonisation of spiritual and temporal. Dario created his own Francis as enthusiastically as had the war-mongering poet of violence Gabriele d'Annunzio, or Victorian religious sceptics like Renan or Matthew Arnold. Fo's Francis had little in common with theirs. He saw him as a revolutionary, a dissident, an independent, a free spirit, an egalitarian, an opponent of privilege, an environmentalist, a lover of nature and of animals, an apostle of peace but also, unexpectedly for a writer so imbued with the secular vision as he was, a man of holiness.

Fo always declared himself an atheist, and was always an adversary of the church as institution, while Francis was a Catholic saint who never wavered in his allegiance to the church. The power, the pomp, the wealth of the church aroused Fo's, and Francis's, ire and Dario raised his voice against the distortions of the gospel which he saw inscribed in current Christian practice and teaching. All throughout his career, he was denounced by Catholic dailies and periodicals including the Vatican daily, *L'Osservatore Romano*, was declared anathema in country pulpits, was denied access by parish priests to halls and meeting places under their control, was attacked for irreverence or blasphemy by the Vatican and by curias all over Italy, and was criticised in Parliament by politicians who saw themselves as representatives of the Catholic faithful. Fo replied forcibly to these attacks, but dissociated himself from those of his colleagues and collaborators who were of a simple, anti-clerical frame of mind, if anti-clericalism involved dismissal of everything associated with traditional, historical Christianity. He was aware that in the history of Christian Europe, the ecclesiastical architecture, the folklore, the art not only of the anonymous masons and designers of the Romanesque and Gothic styles but of the great artists of the Renaissance, were founded on Christian belief. Fo's special contribution to this historical debate was the notion, derived in part from Gramsci, that traditional, religious culture also had social and political implications. In 1969, he argued patiently but tenaciously with members of *Nuova Scena* who failed to see the purpose and relevance of staging medieval sketches about miracles, popes, peasants and *giullari*. Look beneath the religious terms at the culture to see what the Christ figure represents in social and political terms, he told them. At the same time, his youthful Marxist comrade-opponents who believed his interest in religious themes was rooted in something more than history and sociology were not altogether mistaken, as became clear with the passing years. Fo was disturbed by the materialism of popular culture and by the domination of economic values in contemporary society. He had no hesitation in announcing his support for John Paul II not only over such issues as opposition to war but also on bio-engineering. A new interest in the spiritual is evident, and he could not simply leave religious questions aside. The Bolognese Catholic daily, *L'avvenire*, in an unexpectedly favourable review of the monologue on Francis wrote shrewdly that 'the wrath of Fo against the Church has more than anything else revealed that his relationship with the Church cannot be eliminated.'[3] The use of the word "Church" in the second part of the sentence is mistaken, since Fo's enduring relationship was with religion and belief, and his core ethical values were easily compatible with traditional belief. Francis expressed all that Fo most admired in the Christian tradition. If Francis was viewed in his own time as an *alter Christus*, Fo too admired the teaching of Christ as it was set out in the gospels, not as it was embodied by the contemporary church. Francis was viewed in his own time as heterodox because he wished a return to the basic evangelic teaching. Fo was of a similar mind, although he looked not only to the canonical gospels of Matthew, Mark, Luke and John, but also to the more radical, apocryphal gospels. The first manifestation of this conviction was the early one-act play *Il primo miracolo di Gesù* (1977, Jesus' First Miracle), a simple narrative of the infant Christ creating a bird out of clay. The tone was respectful and could not have disturbed a believer, except that the episode came from an apocryphal gospel

Francis was also the author of the first poetry in Italian, and a man who described himself as a jester, God's jester, as Fo states in the introduction to his play. There can be debates on precisely what constitutes a jester or *giullare*,[4] but Fo attributes to Francis the qualities he himself admires and aims to embody:

> ... in the days of Francis, to define oneself a *giullare*, even if in the
> service of God was a deeply provocative act, close to "blasphemy"
> ... He knew the techniques, the trade and the absolute rules of the
> jester's profession. We know from a great number of historians
> that the holy "jester" did not ever deliver sermons in accordance
> with ecclesiastical conventions...

Fo was impressed by one detail recounted by Francis's earliest biographer, Tommaso da Celano, who wrote that his public addresses, even to the Pope, were delivered as a performance in which he employed mime, movement and gestures of his whole body as well as words. Fo's style of acting had always been physical, and at the first performance of his one-man piece on St. Francis in a cloister in Spoleto as part of the *Festival of the Two Worlds*, he moved, declaimed, danced, jumped, pranced and gesticulated against a backdrop decorated with scenes, painted by himself, from the life of the saint. After his stroke, Dario was unsure of his memory, so Franca hovered in the wings as prompter, not merely suggesting lines but intervening in a more homely way to advise him to cover up against the cold as night fell. The fourth wall had long since been beaten down.

One other aspect of Francis's life which appealed to Fo the story-teller was the abundance of colourful, compelling narratives and anecdotes associated with Francis's biography. The number of scenes in Dario's play grew as the work developed, and nine appeared in the printed version. The language of the actual dramatic episodes, but not of the introductions, is an invented mixture of dialects and onomatopoeic sounds. Early scenes recount the youth of Francis, including the demolition of towers, his apprenticeship as stone-mason employed in reconstructing the same towers, his imprisonment after a war, his spiritual crisis and conversion to the religious life and his difficulties with papal authorities over the recognition of his new order. The performance closed with Fo singing Francis's poem *Cantico delle creature* (The Canticle of the Creatures), in a style close to Gregorian chant.

The first scene caused controversy with a Franciscan historian, Tommaso Toschi, who doubted its historical authenticity. It was Fo's belief, backed up by reference to historical sources but denied by the friar,[5] that in Bologna Francis delivered a harangue calling for an end to a war between the city and Imola. No record of the actual words remains, so Fo invented his own version in which the saint ironically, wittily and satirically pretends to exalt war and the death and destruction which are part of armed conflict. The final appeal in this ironic address was to disregard that apostle of peace who was Christ. In an evident reference to recent history, Francis tells his hearers:

> ... there was the war against the Albigensians and the heretical Cathars. Many of you went on this most holy war in obedience to our Holy Pope Innocent who put himself at the head of this just and fearsome crusade ... after this butchery ... many men among you, courageous and religious people, set off for the Holy Land, to war against the infidel. And now what is to be done in this city when it is at peace? Just as well there are the inhabitants of Imola.

Listeners in late 1999 needed no reminding of the wars in Iraq and Afghanistan. That year had also been decreed to be a year of commemoration for the victims of Italy's years of terrorism.

The tale of Francis and the wolf of Gubbio is well known and appears in an early work, *The Little Flowers of St. Francis.* Dario subtly alters the direction of the tale to make it a questioning of human aggression and double-dealing rather than a story of the miraculous taming of a wild animal threatening the people of Gubbio. With the remarkable vocal range he displays in all his monologues, he alternates between the part of the saint and that of the wolf, speaking the wolf's lines in a hoarse, forced, choked voice. The tale is narrated in a style similar to one used for children's stories, like those of Hans Christian Andersen, with a talking wolf justifying its ferocity by referring to the nature with which it was born. Francis remonstrates jovially with the beast: "Hey, that's a good one, that story about nature! With an excuse like that everybody's got a free pass. He can steal, kill, cheat and it's all down to nature." Francis, the wolf and the people of Gubbio reach the agreement that the villagers will feed the wolf and in return it will desist from attacking them. When that settlement has been reached, Francis sets off. Dario inserts a new episode in which villainous monks set their dogs on Francis, but he is rescued by the wolf which had come looking for him to beg to be released from the agreement. The people of Gubbio have been treating him badly, he complains, and feeding him inedible food. The tale of the ravenous wolf of Gubbio is overturned. The danger arises from the incivility of human beings, not the violent instincts of animals. Francis concludes: "I threw myself whole-heartedly into teaching animals to be good people and now

I've got to educate men to become good animals!"

The individual tales which make up this work, with the interludes of violence and savagery which are common in fables and fairy stories, have a charm of their own, but there is a didactic drive, even a philosophy, behind them, again like fairy stories. Fo's Francis is a revolutionary who debates the question reformers have always pondered over whether it is necessary to change individuals to produce a new society, or change society to improve individuals. Francis, and Fo, are convinced it is necessary to change both culture and individual behaviour. His characterisation of Francis represents yet another instance of move from the purely political dimension and gives a new primacy to ethical and cultural questions.

With few exceptions, the Catholic world greeted the work enthusiastically as evidence of the emergence of a 'new' Fo. The Jesuit monthly, *Civiltà cattolica* suggested that he had been touched by "divine grace". Its columnist, Virgilio Fantuzzi, wondered if as Fo was playing St Francis, the saint in heaven had not taken the opportunity to "to take possession of Fo's soul."[6] *L'Avvenire* also ended decades of polemics with Fo by writing that he was "one of the few Italian (and non-Italian) writers to speak of Jesus Christ with a sincerity ... which it is hard to find in a Catholic or so-called Catholic, writer." These were generous critical views, but founded on wishful thinking. Fo had not undergone a conversion of the type experienced by Manzoni or Pascal, but the thought which underlay this work suggested a shift in emphasis and outlook.

Controversy, polemics and disputes came from more predictable quarters following the production of works featuring the business and political career of Silvio Berlusconi. The anti-corruption, *Clean Hands* campaign and the disgrace befalling politicians in the First Republic commanded Fo's attention, and it was 2001 before he produced a work with Berlusconi at the centre, uncompromisingly entitled *Il grande bugiardo* (The Big Liar). Two years later, he delivered what he termed an *oration* in the style of Ruzante, supposedly retelling the plot of Jarry's surreal masterpiece, *Ubu Roi*, but re-titled *Da Tangentopoli all'inarrestabile ascesa di Ubu Bas* (From Bribesville to the Irresistible Rise of Ubu Bas). "It's only a story", he repeated as a refrain in the course of a comic, ironic monologue detailing the problems of the fictional Ubu with the law during his political career, and his skill in manoeuvring a path through obstacles put in his way, however feebly, by legislators. Ubu's career was hampered, or facilitated, by unresolved questions over the separation of powers, as had that of Berlusconi, who commanded a great media empire which gave him control of TV channels as well as of magazines and newspapers, while at the same time leading a political party and becoming the country's Prime Minister. In a liberal democracy, the media are meant to hold politicians to account, but Berlusconi was in a position to enact laws to his own advantage while controlling the means by which information on such activity was conveyed to society. The Ubu story was in two parts, the second entitled *Ubu bas va alla guerra* (Ubu bas Goes to War), a work issued in the days of the Afghan and Iraqi war.[7]

Meantime, he was working on the theatrical piece satirising Berlusconi, *L'anomalo bicefalo* (The Twin-Headed Anomaly). Dario and Franca held open rehearsals in Bagnacavallo, the pretty town in Emilia-Romagna where Byron entrusted his daughter to an order of nuns and where she is buried. The couple planned a nation-wide tour including the Piccolo theatre in Milan, but even before its official opening, the work encountered obstacles with local and national authorities. In October 2003, Sergio Escobar, temporary director of the theatre, wrote in *Corriere della Sera* that he was having difficulties with the theatre's board of management. No one in the theatre had actually read the script, which was still a work in progress, but it was being whispered in the corridors that it might just possibly be unwise, ill-advised, tactless, a failure of diplomatic nous to accept such a politically sensitive work, would it not? Perhaps Dario could be persuaded to submit the work to the theatre for prior approval by more discreet spirits who could offer him advice? The article caused a storm in the press, with most columnists focusing on questions of the limits and acceptability of satire. The real issue was a return of censorship which had been officially abolished years previously.

The tour went ahead, but when it was underway, Senator Marcello Dell'Utri, Berlusconi's right hand man both in his business and political dealings, raised a legal action against Fo and Rame, claiming he had been defamed and demanding in damages the enormous sum of one million euros. The couple regarded the action as an attempt to intimidate them and to pressurise theatres where the play was scheduled for performance to cancel. While the court hearing was still pending, there occurred an event which was more grotesque and absurd than anything even Fo could have invented. The play was due to be broadcast on a network of local and satellite channels on 27 March, but Dell'Utri issued a threat to the companies which planned to air it. The chief company was Planet, an associate of Sky, who bowed to pressure but reached the incredible compromise that the play would be televised, but without sound. Performances not seen since the invention of the talkies were broadcast on Italian TV in the twenty-first century. The actors could be seen on screen moving and talking, but the audience could not hear a word. A few days later, after public protests and a series of incredulous or mocking articles, the company changed its mind and the play was transmitted in the standard way. What made the ban more unbelievable was the fact that the play had been on tour for almost a year before the date scheduled for TV broadcast, and had been seen in all the main theatre centres of Italy. Its contents had been reported and discussed by reviewers and columnists. If any proof was needed of the power of the mass media, Senator Dell'Utri provided it. He was indifferent to theatre, but apprehensive of the power of the television. After delays, the case was heard in court where Dell'Utri's case was dismissed. By that time, Franca had been elected to the Italian senate, making her a colleague of Dell'Utri.

As had happened with earlier plays by Dario, for instance *Accidental Death of an Anarchist,* the play was rewritten during the run to take in new developments or scandals. One such was the Parmalat affair, a scandal that engulfed the Parma-based milk-processing firm owned by the Tanzi family, who were also sponsors of Formula One racing cars and owners of the city's football team. They had previously been regarded as examples of financial probity and business shrewdness, but in 2003, a hole in its accounts of some 14 billion was discovered. Enquiries led to the identification of shadowy offshore companies, the revelation of a series of interlinked frauds and ultimately to a series of court cases which involved European and American banks. This affair provided the cue for Dario to write in various jibes on financial-political intrigue, but the core of *The Twin-Headed Anomaly* was a satirical assault on the emergence of Berlusconi in politics, and of the consequences of *berlusconismo*, the Italian version of late capitalism, on society. While not Fo's most accomplished or imaginative work of satire, it gave a dystopian view of a society in decline, corrupted by a culture and an ethic which was the reverse of that preached by St Francis. The play was always a work in progress, but it was also paradoxically a kind of Selected Works by Fo, incorporating many comic devices which he had used over the years – grammelot, the use of the dwarf figure as in *Fanfani rapito* (1975, The Kidnapping of Fanfani), the transfer of brains and bodies as in *Clacson, trombette e pernacchi* (1981, Trumpets and Raspberries), the use of electroshock treatment, the double ending as in *Accidental Death* and others. In *The Twin-Headed Anomaly*, a director, played by Dario, plans to make a satirical film of Berlusconi and signs up an actress, Franca Rame. At the same time, Berlusconi himself is entertaining Vladimir Putin in Sicily, where they are attacked by a criminal gang, leaving the two men alive but badly injured and requiring complex emergency surgery. All does not go well, and in the course of the operation part of Putin's brain and memory is implanted into Berlusconi's skull. Since Berlusconi's own memory has completely failed, his wife Veronica has to remind him of his past activities – of how he had built up his business empire Fininvest, of the source of the funding for Milano 2, the housing scheme on the outskirts of Milan which was his first commercial venture and whose financing had always been controversial, of his relations with Socialist leader Bettino Craxi and of how that friendship had been invaluable to him when the High Court had ruled illegal his ownership of national TV networks, and of his membership of the mysterious, high-powered Masonic Lodge, the P2, whose covert political programme was curiously similar to many aspects of Berlusconi's own policies in government. However, since the reconstructed Berlusconi has the brains of Putin, an ex-communist, he threatens to implement pseudo-Marxist policies, including the repeal of the laws he had passed in his own favour, a proposal which terrifies his sycophantic allies who have recourse to further electro-therapy treatment to bring him back to what he was.

In part due to the controversy aroused by Dell'Utri and the management of *Il Piccolo*, the play was a great success and the run in the *Piccolo* in January 2004 was a sell-out. The critical reception was more mixed. The complex structure, in which Dario and Franca play themselves, then Berlusconi and his wife and finally the director and actor, did not always work in dramatic terms, but that was hardly the main point. Dario may have used some of these devices previously, but they are freshly developed with an intriguing and involving wit, and linked with uncamouflaged, satiric violence. The treatment meted out to Putin and Berlusconi is not whimsical or escapist, and calls into play all the violence that underlies Fo's comic vision. The two are subjected to a savagery which releases the intensity of the feelings they arouse in writer and spectator. The play ends when the original, fictional director intervenes to say he has recorded all the conversations and will make them available by putting them on the web. This was not a play destined for posterity, nor even likely to be understood in other countries, but gives expression to the bitter, outraged denunciation of one man, one situation, one abuse of power in one age in one country, Italy. Marcello Dell'Utri had at least the merit of recognising the inner nature and force of the play.

Dario used similar situations and ironic devices to lambast Berlusconi in the series of episodes which make up the prose work, *Il paese dei misteri buffi* (The Land of the Comic Mysteries), co-authored with Giuseppina Manin. The key to the situation is that Berlusconi, after visiting the tomb in Arcore, the villa in Milan he had designed for himself, goes missing. On his reappearance, he declares to an incredulous public that he had been kidnapped by devils and taken on a Dantean journey to hell where he met up with other figures from recent Italian political history, including Christian Democrat politicians Aldo Moro, Giulio Andreotti and Francesco Cossiga, as well as the Sicilian Financier Michele Sindona whose activities embarrassed the Vatican and who inspired some scenes in *The Godfather III,* and the head of P2, Licio Gelli. Berlusconi is disbelieved and is locked up in jail, where he passes the time explaining to other inmates the stories he had heard in the underworld about the scandals which rocked political life in Italy from World War II onwards. He does not complain of his main misfortune in life, being a contemporary of Dario Fo.

REFERENCES

1   Dario Fo, *Ubu Roi – Ubu bas*, distributed with La Repubblica, January, 2010.

2   Dario Fo, *Lu santo jullàre Francesco*, Turin, Einaudi, 1999; *L'anomalo bicefalo*, supplement to the periodical, MicroMega, 2/2004

3   *L'Avvenire*, 10 July 1999.

4   Antonio Scuderi, *Unmasking the Holy Jester Dario Fo*, in Theatre Journal, 2003, pp.275-90,

5   *Il Corriere della Sera*, 2 agosto 1999.

6   *La Repubblica*, 17 September 1999.

7   The two talks were issued on a DVD with *La Repubblica*, January 2010.

Chapter 6

FRANCA RAME: LOVE AND DEATH

To many observers, it was strange that the Nobel Prize was not jointly awarded to Dario and Franca, as it had been to Marie and Pierre Curie in 1903. Dario himself recognised the strength of this argument, and said as much in his official address in Stockholm. The speech was not fully written out in advance but delivered from notes and sketches, which were later distributed. One page contained a sketch, based on Raphael's *Lady with a Unicorn*, of Franca holding a friendly animal which may have been a unicorn, but without a horn. It was an affectionate portrait, and the following page depicted a male, arms outstretched, standing upright on the back of a female who was crouched on all fours, an ironic depiction of Franca's wistful statement that she was accustomed to being the pedestal supporting the great man. In the final version of her play, *Grasso è bello* (2001, Fat is Beautiful) the protagonist Mattea complains that she had been married for thirty years to her "dear, quasi Nobel Winner of a husband" and that over time he had become "important ... oh so important! A monument! But a monument, as everybody knows, stands upright on pedestal."[1] Dario's caption over his drawing reads, "I am in training", although the wording leaves it unclear who is undergoing the training, Dario or Franca. There is no such ambiguity to the words at the foot of the page, "Without her, I would not have won." She actually considered renouncing the trip to Stockholm, since she was touring with Giorgio Albertazzi in a play on the unfolding corruption scandal, *Il diavolo con le zinne* (1997, The Devil with Tits). As a seasoned professional, she held to the old adage that the show must go on and the audience never let down. Dario gave her an ultimatum: if she did not go, he would not go either. In the end, they chartered a plane which allowed her respect her schedule and arrive in time for the ceremony.

The play itself was set in the years of the Counter-Reformation and the

Inquisition, in a town where various civic buildings were being burned down and replaced by banks or palaces. A magistrate of unquestioned integrity is summoned to investigate allegations of corruption and malpractice. The local notability, in their campaign to frustrate his enquiries, call on a couple of mischievous devils, one of whom creeps into the magistrate's body by the most secret orifice, thereby changing his personality. The other makes a more dignified entrance into the body of the woman, enhancing her already highly desirable attributes, including the 'tits' of the title. Thus equipped, she ensnares the magistrate, who after assorted misadventures ends up as a galley slave. It was all familiar Fo territory, including a scatological scene where the cardinal sits down to a dinner of horse manure gathered for him by the magistrate.

The authorship of the comedy is attributed to "Dario Fo with the collaboration of Franca Rame," and the play was dedicated to her. The question of her contribution to the writing of the couple's theatre will be discussed as long as their work is deemed worthy of performance. Both have made contradictory statements, some times claiming more credit than was probably due and at others modestly giving all praise to the other. It is not a question that can be resolved by routine feminist rhetoric, that the male suppresses the work of the female, as is now believed to be the case with Bertolt Brecht and Margarete Steffin, at least for many works attributed to him. Franca was scarcely a suppressed female, but in public her image was intimately tied to Dario's. As she repeated on many occasions, the two cooperated on all fronts personally and professionally, so that at times the one was genuinely unsure in retrospect of how much the other had contributed to a shared project. At what point did a helpful criticism made by Franca of an early version of a play by Dario become an act of creativity, which changed the nature of a scene, a dialogue, a character, or even the direction of the text? As she has said herself:

> I intervene at the moment of the 'audit,' if I can put it that way. The difficulty lies in establishing collaboration between the two of us. What happens? Dario sits down to write a play and he gives me every page he writes. Usually, I found myself in the position of giving criticism, or least of making some suggestions. At the beginning I did not have the authority I later gained with the passing of time, above all with *He had Two Pistols and White and Black Eyes.* That was a work where, when I read it, I felt it did not work ... we went on stage at the Odeon in Milan. The play was a success but not the success we expected ... I remember when we were in the

green room, Dario handed me the script and said, "Make the cuts you suggested."[2]

If Franca suggested to Dario ideas for the 1970s monologues on the condition of women and these suggestions were then given full theatrical form by Dario, to whom should authorship be credited? Moreover, in his oration at her funeral, Dario announced that her part in the authorship of the plays was greater than had been admitted, and even suggested that he might have denied this fact out of jealousy. He also said that she was the real author of *Coppia aperta* (1983, Open Couple), something both of them had previously denied. It certainly conflicts with a version he gave to me when he said he had written the play during a tense period in their relationship, but had not really intended it for performance. It was given a private reading to a close circle of friends including Carlo Barsotti, who was then based in Sweden and who had produced several of Fo's plays in translations by his Swedish wife, Anna. He asked permission to stage it in Stockholm, and only after its success there did Dario think of presenting it in Milan. Franca took the principal part in a play, a comedy which show the male character's delight and his wife's dismay at the opportunities afforded by the anti-bourgeois concept of the 'open couple,' until she turns the tables by taking a lover. The work was considered too outrageous for the Italian Ministry who banned under 18 year olds from attending.

Franca was never an anonymous or background figure, but at times the lack of full recognition seems to have irked her. In 1999, she gave Giuseppina Manin an interesting interview which revealed more of the couple's private life than she was normally prepared to divulge. It was published under a title chosen by the sub-editors, "How Tiring to Live Under the Shadow of Fo,"[3] and in it Franca gave vent to her feelings on a variety of items, domestic, personal and authorial. At home, the couple had decided that it was politically incorrect to employ a servant, but she found herself living with "two men: a disorderly son and a husband whose mother even used to put on his socks. One day I got fed up and pinned a notice on the wall of the living room; from today on, anyone who wishes to eat or to have his shirts ironed can do it himself." She had to add that "to avoid chaos, I had to put my principles to one side and hire a fantastic Filipino maid". These domestic arrangements are interesting enough, although they did have trouble with later Filipinos who were less fantastic. Domestic servants of various nationalities became a fixture in the Fo-Rame household, which became increasingly crowded as secretaries and assistants were taken on to help with an increasingly heavy work load. The

Fo house in Milan, as more than one journalist noted, was in a state of permanent creative disorder. Dario worked, with his clerical and artistic helpers, in a flat downstairs from their home, where some canvases were left leaning in piles against the walls, some sketches pinned to boards, and works in progress were supported on easels.

Franca supervised the task of putting all the works, including successive edits, on-line, but she also continued humanitarian work, giving well paid and rewarding work to prisoners. She got inmates to do much of the uploading when she had their joint archive put on a website where all reviews, interviews and successive drafts of the plays are available. She attended to correspondence, taking bookings, looking after management tasks and overseeing the final editing needed before a play could be viewed as suitable for publication. Dario was happy with this arrangement, and rarely dissented. "Fai tu (You do it)," were the words she said she heard most frequently from him. The implication was that he would trust her totally, but also that he would have no need to concern himself unduly with mundane matters. She also issued a regular blog. In the same interview, Franca moved on to her role as archivist, defining it as "my real profession", and it is beyond dispute that future producers and researchers will be in her debt. The invention of the computer made this task easier and in the years following the award of the Nobel Prize she spent much time seated in front of a computer, editing their work.

In the interview with Manin, under the heading *Author*, Franca made the bald statement, "Of the one hundred plays written by Dario, we wrote half of them together. I am his consultant, a thankless role. It is necessary to tell the truth." Perhaps there is no simple truth. Perhaps their collaboration was so close that it is not possible to identify individual contribution. The principal creative contribution and impulse in the vast majority of cases was Dario's, but that does not mean that Franca's part is to be downplayed or that at times she does not deserve the title author. It is interesting to look at the successive ways authorship is acknowledged in the volumes which were to make up their Collected Works, published by Einaudi. (The series ends in 1998 with volume XIII when the company was bought over by Berlusconi. The couple broke off dealings with this publisher, and later works were published elsewhere.) The first twelve volumes were published as *Le commedie di Dario Fo*, although for volume XI and XII, the title page carried the rubric, "edited by Franca Rame." Volume XIII was issued under the title *Le commedie di Dario Fo e Franca Rame* and included the double bill, *Grasso è bello* (Fat is Beautiful) and *Eroina*

(Heroine/Heroin). These two works were initially together published in 1991, the year the second play was staged in Ravenna, by Kaos Edizioni as *Parliamo di donne* (Let's Talk about Women) with Franca Rame's name alone as author on the cover, but both names together in an inside page. Franca not only performed the principal role but was also main author of *Fat is Beautiful* and sole author of *Heroin/Heroine*. As she said at an earlier stage in her life in a reply to a question from an interviewer from *L'Unità* who asked how she felt about writing a work on her own, "I think I've succeeded in expressing the concepts I wanted to. I can die happy, don't you agree?"[4] On the authorship of *Fat is Beautiful*, she later explained the procedure more simply. "The script was written by me. After that, Dario came along and added his mark of genius."[5] The creative process is easier to follow for these plays since the comments and successive versions are available on the Fo-Rame website. The plays had undergone the customary process of joint discussion, comment, rewriting and discussion in rehearsal, but it is clear that in this case the original inspiration was Franca's. When asked how important her contribution had always been, she replied:

> I bear no rancour towards Dario, because at the basis of everything there's my biggest failing – that of having no ambition. It's not that Dario ever thought, "Franca will provide me with ideas and I'll look smart!" No, that never crossed his mind. If I hadn't been his wife, if I'd been somebody else, he would of necessity had to put my name too as author. Einaudi published numerous scripts by Dario all edited by me, and initially there was not even the acknowledgement "edited by Franca Rame." When I asked Roberto Cerati for an explanation, he said, "We just never thought of it." The problem is that I am the *wife*, and a wife sometimes is a piece of domestic furniture.[6]

As in the other plays on the condition of women, the central character in *Fat is Beautiful* is again the mother-figure, Mattea. Engaged in a struggle to come to terms with desertion by her husband and the indifference of her daughter, she gorges herself with gargantuan quantities of food, becoming enormously obese. As she lies in bed, a male voice speaks gentle, caressing words to her, but the words are pre-recorded, not spoken by a living man. A psychoanalyst, in an effort to raise her self-esteem, advises prostitution as a means of persuading herself of her enduring attractiveness, but she finds comfort only with her virtual lover. Franca produced two versions of this work, cutting out redundant characters in the second and reducing the piece to a near-monologue. She had to perform with padding around her middle, to make her appear as fat as her character. It was a bitter comedy, depicting a woman starved of affection, devoid of any sense of self-worth, and the work appeared empty of all hope of changing the condition if not of women, at least of this woman.

This work relied on the comic grotesque which Franca and Dario had employed for years, but *Heroine/Heroin* was conceived and written in a different style. The work was Franca's, although Dario collaborated fully in discussions, rewriting, directing and staging. He had reservations about it. When the possibility of reviving it was raised in later years, he could not be persuaded that it was worthwhile and the proposal was dropped. His objection was that the work was too monotone, too unvaried, too consistently dark and lacking in episodes of irony. It is unquestionably the blackest play in the Fo-Rame canon, more similar to monologues written by Samuel Beckett than to any previous work produced by either of them. Comedy, including grotesque comedy, is discarded and the action unfolds in a bleak urban wasteland, where acts of savage, gratuitous violence are commonplace.

The inspiration came from real events in Bologna, and the title expresses a grim pun between the two meanings of the word, heroin and a heroic woman. Carla, the mother, known also as *mater tossicorum*, has already seen two of her children die, one of a heroin overdose and the other of Aids. She declaims against an unseen God, and rages that her determination to save her third daughter, also an addict, has led her to lock her up at home, while she herself, having seen other addicts die from using contaminated substances, has turned to prostitution to raise the funds to buy pure, unadulterated, heroin. Her hope is eventually to take her surviving daughter to Liverpool where, she believes, enlightened detoxification and therapeutic policies were being practiced. There are references to contemporary Italian politicians, such as Rosa Russo Jervolino, who had taken what Franca viewed as a reactionary line on sex education, but the other characters are identified only by symbolic names such as the blind man or the deaf mute, and could emerge from some metaphysical dimension. The landscape is bleak, and the violence random, with shots fired by unknown assailants ringing out. It is a powerful, inexplicably neglected piece of theatre, and the part she played permitted Franca to express herself as a dramatic, serious actress. The brutality of the plot caused upset and some theatres refused to accept a booking, but even critics who were doubtful about the work were impressed by Franca's performance.

In addition to writing and acting, Franca continued her humanitarian efforts in various spheres of society. The Nobel Prize money amounted to a massive 1,650,000,000 lire, and the Fos decided to establish what they called the Nobel for the Disabled and to distribute the entire sum to handicapped people and to organisations dedicated to working with them. Franca dedicated herself energetically to the task and managed to persuade Volkswagen to contribute to the fund. The takings from shows which the Fos produced, as well as from sales of prints and sketches by Dario, were also gifted to the cause. Requests were invited from deserving causes, but in this sad and tainted world some applications turned out to be fraudulent or completely bogus. A committee was set up to examine requests, and an accountant, Luciano Silva, was appointed to head the organisation. Silva seemed a man of the utmost integrity, and gained the trust of his colleagues. When the organisation was fully functional, some well publicised events were arranged and donations made to several charities, with the gift of equipment, machines and Volkswagen mini-buses being particularly appreciated.

Regrettably, by mid 2004, Franca began to have suspicions that there was something awry in the administration of the fund, and that some moneys were not being used for the intended purpose. Investigations revealed that a large sum had been paid from an account which had been closed some years previously, and suspicion fell on Silva. A pattern of systematic fraud to his own benefit was uncovered, and advertisements were placed in national newspapers to announce that he had been dismissed and no longer represented the committee. When the case went to court in September 2006, it was revealed that the sum involved amounted to almost 400,000. The next hearing took place in May 2007, and on this occasion Dario and Franca took advantage of a provision of Italian law which permits injured parties to be represented directly, as *parte civile*. Silva's lawyers proposed a bargain, which would have seen him repay €50,000 and serve a sentence of one year and four months. Discussions over repayment were inconclusive and in July the court was told that Silva did not have the money to make reparation. The case was concluded in November when Silva was sentenced to two and half years' imprisonment and to a repayment of €200,000 to the fund, although this would require further civil action. The court also ordered payment of € 20,000 to the bank. In a statement, Dario said he was satisfied with the outcome, although puzzled that the bank was recognised as a wronged party. Franca's health suffered from the stress of the lengthy, bitter proceedings, and she had to receive medical treatment and cancel some performances. She and Dario had behaved with great generosity and magnanimity, but had been cheated. So too had the disabled they had attempted to assist.

Meantime, Franca had to face another legal case of her own, this time brought against her by Roberto Castelli, a member of the Northern League and Minister for Justice in the coalition government headed by Silvio Berlusconi. In 2002, the minister had expressed bewilderment over a hunger strike by prisoners, since in his view "prison is comparable to a five-star hotel." This statement outraged Franca, who had been campaigning for prison reform since establishing in 1972 the organisation *Soccorso Rosso* (Red Aid), whose aim was to offer legal and humanitarian assistance to activists who had been imprisoned for participation in the demonstrations which shook Italy in those years. She excluded those who advocated the use of violence. In a demonstration outside the Regina Coeli prison in Rome, she called the minister "un pirla," a term of abuse which could be rendered in English as "prick," but which, like its English equivalent, has transmogrified into a generic insult. Castelli is obviously a sensitive soul and claimed the term was defamatory. He raised an action, demanding 100,000 in damages. The case was settled in July 2005, with a symbolic award of 3,000. The judge noted that the word "pirla" was a dialect word and that its use had not been reported in all the media covering the event.

These vexations aside, Franca's life was about to change radically. In early 2006, while Dario was still campaigning for nomination as Leftist candidate for mayor of Milan, she was invited to stand for the senate as an independent in the lists of *Italia dei Valori* (Italy of Values), a centre-left party founded in 1998 by Antonio Di Pietro. The ex-magistrate, whose anti-corruption campaign had been fully backed by Dario and Franca, entered political life in 1996, and set up his own party two years later. As the high-sounding name suggests, the party's main aim was the ethical reform of public life in Italy, and it quickly became a thorn in the side of Berlusconi. The invitation to Franca was promoted by Leoluca Orlando, mayor of Palermo, who had had long admired her work and had granted her honorary citizenship of the city in 2000 in recognition of her activities for the disadvantaged. The initiative received support from Di Pietro, but Franca, who was now 77, initially hesitated. Dario too was doubtful, worried that the strain and the constant travelling would be too much for her. She had already been candidate for the Milan City Council in 2001, but election to the senate would involve demands of an altogether different order. She took soundings among her friends, while her son Jacopo did an online consultation, and the consensus was that she should accept the nomination. The decision was made public at the end of February. As is possible under electoral law in Italy, she headed the party's list of candidates in six regions, Veneto, Piedmont, Lombardy, Tuscany, Emilia-Romagna and Umbria. Her decision caused some annoyance in the ranks of Communist Refoundation, which had been Dario's main supporter in his mayoral campaign, but Franca replied simply that *Italia dei valori* was a party of the Left adding, "I am standing for Di Pietro's party because he has blown the system up in the air and has made Italians smile."[7] The same justification, of finding some force capable of blowing the system sky-high, would be used years later to explain support for Beppe Grillo and his movement.

Jacopo prepared colourful, striking manifestos which established the main points of Franca's campaign. Some carried political commitments – "I will use my salary as senator to raise awareness of state waste. No more tossing public money out the window!" while another was a powerful slogan against rape – "No excuses for rape." Franca's appeal to women voters was conveyed in a cartoon with a balloon coming from her mouth with the words, "Women of Italy show courage! Seek your own representation. A woman for women." Underneath there was an attractive rhyme, *Se di questa Italia sei stanca / il 9 aprile vota per Franca* (It you're tired of this Italy / On 9 April vote for Franca.) Negative campaigning, as American pollsters have discovered, has its value, so other posters depicted Berlusconi in convict uniform, dressed as Putin or else announcing – "In the last 10 years, I've made €10b. How did you get on?"

Franca proposed a strong programme of radical reforms. Obviously she was moved by deep antagonism to Berlusconi, both for the laws he had introduced to defend his own interests and for the neo-liberal, anti-Welfare policies his government had implemented. Support for the anti-war movement too was a central theme in her candidacy. She declared herself in favour of bringing back the soldiers from Iraq, although this stance would create some tactical problems for her later. Her platform included a drive to revive the anti-corruption Clean Hands campaign which was losing strength, encouragement for the movement to increase the numbers of women in elected positions and greater funding for the protection of the environment. Perhaps the distinctive feature of her campaign was her vociferous outrage at the waste of public resources, evidenced in the management of the state, the useless expenditure of national income on

grandiose but worthless schemes, the sheer inefficiency, or worse, of bureaucratic practice, the tolerance of tax evasion and the ineffectiveness
of a court system which allowed wealthy criminals to escape justice. She
proposed a more energetic drive against financial fraud and the privileges enjoyed by those who were elected supposedly as servants of the people
- all factors she and Dario had exposed and denounced in their theatre.
The alienation of Italians from the state and its representatives, together
with the cynicism which resulted from it, seemed to her to flow from institutional injustice and to represent a danger to democracy. She promised to use the salary due to her as senator to subsidise a push against
waste and inefficiency at every level of the Italian state.

After the initial excitement had subsided, she found it hard to get her
voice heard in the noise of an election campaign, so she took paid advertisements in newspapers. Her electioneering was completed with a
performance of the anti-Iraq war monologue on Cindy Sheehan which
had already been produced in London. Plainly her appeal resonated with
voters, because on the 9 April she was elected with over 500,000 votes
in Piedmont. "I found myself elected without having lifted a finger," she
wrote in her autobiography,[8] although she later put it even more strongly
when she said she had done all she could so as *not* to be elected. The Centre-Left recorded a victory and Romano Prodi, to whom Franca felt a high
degree of personal affinity and loyalty, became Prime Minister.

The victory was exhilarating for her supporters, but for Franca herself it
was to prove the high point of what was to be a bitter personal experience.
She remained a senator only until January 2008 when she resigned, but almost from her arrival in Palazzo Madama she was telling journalists that
she was tired, disillusioned, exasperated and unhappy. "I felt like an eight-
een-year of bride married off to a man she does not love," was the colourful
expression quoted in several newspapers. Her early days made her feel as
though she had been "catapulted into Uganda, without knowing the language, without knowing where to go or who to talk to."[9] Uganda was chosen
at random, but her reference to finding herself unexpectedly in an African
country whose way were totally unfamiliar to her is significant. Franca was
plainly disoriented in the Roman senate, and her later chronicles of events
read like a report written by an anthropologist studying the ways of an ex-
otic and not particularly sympathetic tribe in some foreign land of which he
knows little. Not even in retrospect could she reconcile herself to the time
in the senate, which she described as "the refrigerator of feelings. Never a
smile in that building, and solitude you cannot imagine. Nineteen months

of imprisonment, the worst in my life."[10]

Franca published two separate accounts of her life as senator, one in the final pages of the episodic autobiographical work which is credited as being co-authored with Dario, *Una vita all'improvvisA* (An Improvised Life). She meditated on her experiences at greater length in a book which she was credited as having written by herself, *In fuga dal senato* (In Flight from the Senate.) The image on the cover, designed by Dario, shows a disconcerted Franca seated uncomfortably on an old-style bicycle with flowers in baskets before and behind her. Her hands are in the air, and the bicycle is free-wheeling. Dario used this book as the basis for a theatrical monologue which he performed all over Italy in Franca's honour after her death.[11]

It was a bitter work, written by a deeply disenchanted woman. She who could face audiences of thousands with tranquillity was intimidated by the solemn impersonality of the senate, the hollowness of the rituals, and by details like the routine salutes of the guards whom she was not expected to greet in their turn.

She writes that on the day of her initiation into the senate, being unable to sleep, she wandered about Rome in the early hours when the city was still asleep. She found herself in front of the senate building, Palazzo Madama

> Leaning on a wall facing it, I observe the palace with a feeling of emptiness in my stomach. Maybe I am hungry. I have not found a bar open. My God, I really have to go in there. What's waiting for me? I am really agitated.[12]

In the following days, she found herself bursting into tears outside the Teatro Argentina, wondering if she was in the company of a tribe of Indians in the Rockies or had fallen down the rabbit hole like Alice in Wonderland. She was deeply offended by the refusal of parliamentarians, especially women whom she had previously known and to whom she had shown kindliness and friendliness, to acknowledge her presence. The fact that she would have to meet face to face politicians like Marcello Dell'Utri, who had sued her and Dario, or Giulio Andreotti, whom they had satirised and derided decade after decade, dismayed her. Curiously, these two men both behaved with courtesy, even with old-school gallantry. Dell'Utri made himself known to her, asking her if she recognised him, and whispering to her that she need have no worry about the one million euros he was seeking as damages for the injury to his reputation.

She replied that they were not at all worried, as she was sure the case would go nowhere. "I have many lawyers," was his delphic reply. Andreotti displayed the personal touch towards her, albeit in his characteristically patrician and condescending manner. He was Chair of a meeting Franca had to attend, and when he saw her he greeted her with the words, "*Piccina*, your smile illuminates the senate." Piccina means approximately "little girl," but was seemingly spoken with warmth not disdain, thereby throwing Franca off guard for the moment. She rallied and tried to engage him in conversation on the kidnap of Aldo Moro and why the Christian Democrat government had refused to enter negotiations with the Red Brigades for the release of their president. Andreotti replied it would have undermined the state to have given equal dignity to the *Brigate Rosse*, and when Franca objected that they could have saved the life of a human being, his reply was to stretch out his arms.

It was less than a month before she was embroiled in her first public controversy, with ex-minister for Health, Francesco Storace. He had been forced to resign from Berlusconi's government when implicated, although later acquitted, in a scandal which went under the name Laziogate, involving the misappropriation of public funds by the right-wing regional council of Lazio. She was quoted in the press as saying that she would have liked to tell Storace, "cross your arms so you can get used to handcuffs." These remarks would have been greeted with laughter in theatre, but she was now a parliamentary deputy and found herself arraigned in the national press for a lapse in style. It would not be the last time she made personal, ironic criticism nor the last time she would find the whole establishment lined up against this outsider. There was no shortage of other issues to arouse her scorn. She was enraged when during a debate on the massacre of Italian soldiers in Iraq, some senators failed to behave with due gravitas and were seen laughing and joking. However, she had not alienated everyone, and somewhat to her dismay discovered she was proposed for the position of President of the Republic. Voting is carried out by a specially convened college of all deputies and senators together with a selection of representatives of city and regional councils. The first round of voting took place on 9 May. She received 24 votes, more than any other woman candidate, but a low enough vote to let her off the hook.

The procedures of the legislature seemed to her more farcical than anything she and Dario had ever devised. She compared the situation in parliament to the plot of Ben Jonson's satirical comedy, *Bartholomew Fair*, where, she said, "there was no difference between normality and madness."[13] The exposure to party politics with all the infighting, compromise, tangled negotiations, conflicts dictated by self-interest or naked ambition rather than principle appalled her. She was not exactly an innocent abroad and had witnessed bitter ideological struggles, double dealings, deception and mendacity between rival groups when she and Dario had been part of the companies, *Nuova Scena* and later *La Comune*, which they had established in the late 1960s, but if her experiences of life had left her free of any trace of naivety, she entered the senate with a determination and candour of mind and outlook which were among her most attractive characteristics. They were severely tested. Her accounts bring to mind another English work, John Bunyan's *Pilgrim's Progress*. Her words are a record of humiliations, of disappointment and frustration and of deceits perpetrated on her. On one occasion some three hundred and seventy-four amendments to a Bill were proposed in her name, but with her signature forged. Another disappointment was with the conduct of her colleagues towards their own employees. Enquiries revealed that it was the custom of members to engage their assistants without giving them proper contracts and without passing on to them the full amount made available by Parliament for the payment of secretaries or researchers. Franca did not make herself popular with deputies and senators when she revealed these practices and other abuses of privileges, such as subsidised visits to the hair dressers, cheap meals, coffees or the overuse of official cars or planes.

She had an early mishap when she pressed the wrong button on a vote on a tax measure, but she showed her determination to make a difference and to implement the policies she had advocated. She failed with a motion to reduce the expenses provided to political parties, but she issued a blog which had many followers and which drew attention to practices followed across party lines. A motion presented on refinancing the Italian mission in Afghanistan presented her with a moral challenge of a different, deeper order. Franca had campaigned in favour of withdrawing the Italian forces from the country, but any defeat of the motion was likely to lead to the resignation of Prime Minister Romano Prodi and the return to power of Berlusconi. Franca was faced with a dilemma concerning the clash between moral ideals and political reality expressed centuries before by Machiavelli in the pithy statement that he thought differently when he was in the piazza and when he was in the Palace. In the palace, including Palazzo Madama, a representative had to debate with herself over how power should be wielded, to what end it should be used and how its various outcomes could be reconciled. In the context of this vote, every course of action entailed dangers and every move was unacceptable for reasons of its own. She could not justify to herself voting for the continuing presence of Nato forces in Afghanistan, but nor could she face the consequences of casting her vote in a way which would bring down the government and allow Berlusconi access to power once more. Her instincts were to vote with her conscience, but she received messages, from Dario and Jacopo among others, urging her to vote in a way that would keep Berlusconi out. She considered resigning. At the time, she was suffering from a badly sprained ankle and had some difficulty walking. Some malicious articles appeared suggesting that this temporary disability might provide her with a convenient excuse for absenting herself for the vote. In the event, she turned up, took the long view and voted for the renewal of the financing, thus ensuring that Prodi stayed in power – and that the Italian military presence in Afghanistan was maintained.[14]

Her energies were not exclusively taken up with on party business. She organised conferences on reducing waste and on reforming electoral services, introduced bills on such subjects as excluding from office civil servants who had been found guilty of crimes, and on improving health services for soldiers injured in service. With some other senators, she drew up and presented a manifesto containing what became known as the "Ten Laws to Change Italy," publicised in adverts in the national press.[15] The proposals covered such topics as making property seized from the mafia available for socially useful projects, making it easier for citizens to obtain redress when victims of crime and recognising the responsibility of companies for accidents at work. None of them became law, while Franca herself received anonymous death threats, although she was used to that. Her presence in senate seemed to her increasingly futile, and in January 2008 she sent a letter to the President of the senate announcing her intention to resign and explaining at length her dissatisfaction. The Prodi government fell in May. Franca gave her entire salary to a variety of bodies from the Centre for Research into Tumours to the Milan Prosecutor's Office. The latter used the money to buy 20 computers.

Even after her resignation, there was no reduction of her public activities, particularly those involving the struggle against organised crime, against violence on women or against racism. She also campaigned in favour of reform of the drug laws and of prison conditions. At the same time, she was editing volumes which were published under both their names, such as *L'osceno è sacro* (The Obscene is Sacred) or *Correggio che dipingeva appeso in cielo* (Correggio Who Painted Suspended in the Heavens) and many others. In January 2012, she addressed an open letter to Mario Monti, the economist and ex EU Commissioner who in 2011 became head of the "technocratic" government in Rome when all political solutions seemed impossible. In it, she expressed general support for his endeavours but chided him for his failure to introduce reforms to reduce waste, and urged on him greater equity in sharing the burden of remedying the Italian economy after the financial crisis of 2008.

She and Dario went on tour with some scenes from *Mistero buffo,* and Franca assisted in the performance and preparation of a book in homage to Picasso.[16] However, her health was declining and she required greater and greater medical assistance. Late in 2012, she suffered what was described as a minor stroke, which left her weakened. She had to spend more time resting, although she was always willing, probably more than was wise, to offer help when requested. I met her in her home in February to do what turned out to be the last interview she was able to give. Her voice had no longer the vivacity of other times and she was visibly enfeebled. When asked if she had any unfulfilled ambitions in theatre, she replied, "Perhaps now the real aspiration is to rest." She died on 29 May 2013, with Dario and Jacopo at her bedside.

Her death was marked by respectful obituaries in newspapers all round the world, recognising her achievements as actress, writer, political activist and campaigner against social injustice. Her coffin was covered in a red drape and her funeral ceremony held in the open outside the Piccolo Teatro in Milan. In his panegyric, Dario told a story which he said Franca had adapted from an apocryphal version of the Book of Genesis. Eve preceded Adam, and when God spoke to them He offered them the chance to choose to eat the fruit of one of two trees, the first of which would guarantee immortality but the other would bring wisdom and doubt. Eve discovered that the second tree would offer the possibility of love but also the certainty of death. She preferred the chance of finding love, even if it meant mortality and death.

REFERENCES

1   *Le commedie di Dario Fo e Franca Rame*, Turin, Einaudi, 1998, p.54

2   Franca Rame with Joseph Farrell, *Non è tempo di nostalgia*, Pisa, Della Porta editori, 2013, pp81-2.

3   Corriere della Sera, 8 December 1999.

4   Interview with Franca in *L'Unità*, 26 November 1991.

5   *Non è tempo di nostalgia*, cit., pp94-97.

6   *Non è tempo di nostalgia*, cit., p87.

7   *La Stampa*, 28 February 2006.

8   Franca Rame – Dario Fo, *Una vita all'improvvisa*, Parma, Guanda, 2009, p.279.

9   *Libero*, 29 May 2006.

10   *Espresso*, 17 January 2013.

11   *Una vita all'improvvisa*, cit. *In fuga dal senato*, Milan, Chiarelettere, 2013.

12   *In fuga dal senato*, cit., p.22.

13   *Espresso*, cit, p.286.

14   *Il Corriere della Sera*, 23 July 2006.

15   *La Repubblica*, 15 July 2007.

16   Dario Fo, *Picasso Desnudo*, Parma, Guanda, 2012.

Chapter 7

THE SADNESS OF THE CLOWN: LIFE WITHOUT FRANCA

Franca had always said that when she died, Dario would carry on working and writing as before, and so it proved. By the afternoon of her death, he was back at his desk dictating. Certainly the words were related to Franca, and were part of the tribute he distributed to various media outlets in her memory. After the funeral, he resumed writing and performing at the same rate as before. It was not that he was indifferent, and there was certainly nothing callous or unfeeling in his attitude. He carried on because there is no alternative given to human beings in such circumstances. He missed her sorely, and mourned her deeply. Keeping the memory of her alive and supporting the causes she had worked for became one of the mainsprings of his life and activity. Once when asked how he coped with old age, he replied that it would all have been so much easier if Franca had been at his side. "I dream of her. She comes back to me, the last time just a couple of days ago. She gives me advice, even if from a distance."[1]

There was no let-up of Dario's general activity. He continued to hold three times a year in Alcatraz, the estate in Umbria run by their son Jacopo, the seminars on acting which he and Franca had conducted for many years. Visitors were disconcerted by the level of busyness at his home in Milan, where he carried on writing and painting surrounded by actors, stage designers, photographers and young artists. The house was more than ever a lively atelier where the days where spent in research, discussions, writing and consulting manuscripts for his books. Piero Sciotto, a singer-song-writer and actor who had worked with Dario and Franca as performer and administrator since the 1970s, shared with him the writing of a novel on the Sicilian forger, Paolo Ciulla. He described the atmosphere:

> We worked on the book at a distance. It would have been impossible to work elbow to elbow. Dario divides his time between thou-

sands of the most varied tasks – painting above all, which fills in his days and takes up the dead moments between one activity and another. Then, apart from our novel, there's the other writing he has been engaged over the past year, *Lucrezia Borgia, Maria Callas*, the revision of *The Holy Jester Francis* and finally *There is a Mad King in Denimark*, and others underway. Not to mention the productions on tour in Italy and Europe, Franca's *The Flight from the Senate*, for instance. And then there's TV work, the endless meetings and interviews on a wide variety of subjects.

In other words, Dario does not spare himself. He never stops. It was always the same, but even more now when Franca is not there with him.[2]

His political work showed no sign of slowing down, especially now that he had endorsed the policies and campaigns of Beppe Grillo and his 5 Stars Movement. He poured out polemical articles on Italian politics and other subjects, published mainly in a new, independent newspaper, *Il Fatto Quotidiano*, which he was happy to support. He gave speeches in public with the same frequency as ever, championing human rights causes, attacking the new governing establishment but retaining his freedom to be critical of parties and people he supported, that is, Grillo and his Movement. One of the causes which engaged his attention was the treatment of immigrants, whether legal or illegal. He was appalled by the disaster at sea off the coast of Lampedusa when many refugees making the crossing from North Africa in improvised, overcrowded boats were thrown overboard and drowned. Some were saved by Italian coast-guards, but in spite of the efforts of various charities and official bodies, the survivors had to endure dreadful conditions. Dario phoned the mayor of Lampedusa to offer to provide tents at his own expense, but he was told that she could not accept them because the police were dealing with the situation which meant it was outwith her jurisdiction. When he protested at this bureaucratic inhumanity, she outdid satire by replying simply, "we are in Italy." Fo took advantage of his unrestricted access to the press to go public, and the matter was resolved. Around this time, some deputies proposed changes in the law regarding illegal immigrants, and were supported by some elected representatives of the 5 Star Movement. To Dario's dismay, these deputies were then publicly disowned by Grillo. Dario expressed his disagreement with the party leader in public, and expatiated on view that, all humanitarian considerations aside, immigration was good for the Italian economy, since most immigrants were in work and paying taxes.[3]

In October 2013, *Un clown vi seppellirà* (A Clown's Going to Bury You All),[4] co-authored with the journalist Giuseppina Manin, was published. February's General Election had shaken the old order and Grillo's movement, with 163 elected members, was now the third party in Parliament, after the centre-left Democratic Party and Berlusconi's People of Freedom party. While Dario is deeply ill at ease with the neo-liberal beliefs and practices implemented in Italy as elsewhere, and wonders if Italy is facing a crisis of identity and purpose, in the book he adopts a wry, sceptical but generally sanguine attitude towards the possibility of the emergence of a "new" Italy. Could the country be stumbling towards a cultural revolution comparable to 1948 or 1968? Dario had lived through the climate of hope in those moments, and was again with one half of his brain in the grips of one of those moods of optimism, however cautious, to which he was prone. However, he was also deeply schizophrenic in his outlook. At other moments, he sounded dismayed at what had become of all the optimism and grand hopes that had swirled around him and his circle twice in his life, firstly after the Liberation and then in the excitement of the post-68 movement. The victories won then had been undone, the culture was now less promising, the laughter more forced and hollow, the feeling of despair more deep-seated. The political irritant whose jibes and provocations might produce the pearl of change is for him Beppe Grillo, the clown of the title, whose cause is championed in the text by Dario but treated with greater scepticism by Manin. He suggests that Grillo is 'like a character from one of my comedies, a surrealist visionary whose imagination and jokes have at least had the merit of awakening the sleeping country." Dario is incapable of writing in any style other than the ironic, so any hope, however desperate it is, is based on the belief that Italy after putting up with scandals and corruption year after year, may finally be close to some final but cleansing catastrophe. The country is in his view precariously balanced between the longing for change, even revolutionary change, and a yearning for order and stability. The aspiration towards a more orderly version of the status quo is met, in his view, by the overarching governing coalition of Left and Right headed by PM Enrico Letta, but maybe below the surface the old order may be tottering and new forces stirring:

> In fact, 163 Martians have landed in Parliament … And they don't have little green aerials on their heads. They are young, nice, some with degrees, a bit unsure, highly excited. They're all somewhat stunned by their sudden, bumpy landing in another

world, but they're determined to stun the natives in the place, the
ones seated on the public seats that have put down thousand-year
old roots, who consider that court to be their property. In other
words, they're the real UFOs, scruffy in appearance but underneath fearsome and insidious. No sci-fi film had ever imagined
anything like this. Never mind Spielberg. The man of the moment is Beppe Grillo.

It was not easy to establish a stable partnership with a flamboyant, unreliable gadfly like Grillo, who enjoyed being provocative, who issued blogs
and posts on the spur of the moment and who was given to ranting at
great length on public platforms with the risk of losing control. Dario had
never joined a party, unlike Franca who had been for a short time in the
Communist Party. He was as little suited to the discipline of party membership as Groucho Marx, but he has remained of the view that the 5 Star
Movement, warts and all, represents the best vehicle for radical change
in Italy. This has meant that he has received regular calls from journalists
anxious to find out if the latest outburst from Grillo had finally made him
lose patience. He has pulled off the difficult trick of remaining loyal to
his friend while criticising him when he feels it necessary. He remained
relaxed when asked for his reaction to Grillo giving the raised index finger gesture to a female journalist, replying that he had been provoked by
the lies written by many journalists. In February 2014, in response to the
introduction by the government of a guillotine to restrict discussion on
important measures, some 5 Star deputies stormed the speaker's chair in
Parliament, shouting sexist slogans as they did so. Dario called them to
order and invited them to respond to objectionable measures with irony
and imagination. On another occasion, he advised Grillo, who was known
to be considering an anti-EU coalition with UKIP in the European parliament and was seen dining with Nigel Farage, to proceed with caution. His
reaction was remarkably mild. He admitted he knew little about Farage,
and his experience in Italy led him to be sceptical about information
picked up only in the press. "I trust Grillo and Casaleggio, but Farage has
different values," he said.[5]

Autumn 2013 saw Dario in Genoa for the first stop on his tour with his
work on Franca's experiences in the senate. He took the opportunity to
visit Marassi prison where builders with the assistance of the prisoners had constructed a theatre on an empty space inside the prison walls.
While happy to applaud the scheme, he used the inaugural event to con-

demn the prison system as one of the fifty plagues of Italy. In the same city in December, he appeared on a platform with Grillo for his third *Vaffa Day*. His official theme was culture and the position of working people, but he ranged widely, delivering a rebuke to the left-wing parties for their tardiness in denouncing the escape of gases over Taranto from an industrial complex, reiterating his objections to the project to build a tunnel for the High Speed train in the Val di Susa and once again calling for action to alleviate the plight of desperate refugees in Italy. However, a fellow satirist, Vauro Senesi, a friend who had taken part in many campaigns with him, took exception to Fo's views, or perhaps to the company in which he expounded them and wrote an open letter inviting Fo to "get down from the stage." The reply he received for his trouble showed that Fo, although he wrote in tones of hurt incomprehension over a lost soulmate, had still had a command of acerbic sharpness when offended. He wondered why Vauro had neglected all the other themes he had discussed and on which they had campaigned together, and why he had fixed especially on a phrase used by Beppe Grillo. In jeering at the coalition government in Rome, Grillo had raised his voice, as he was wont to do, to yell from Genoa to the capital, "You're all dead, corpses." Vauro, somewhat stretching the point, detected in this an echo of the Fascist worship of death, and invited Dario to dissociate himself from it. In reply, Dario gave him a lesson on the intrinsic ferocity of irony in history and on the necessary offensiveness intrinsic to satire, referring to scenes from Lucian of Samosata, Dante, *commedia dell'arte* and *Hamlet* in which death is portrayed with savagery for purposes of satire. In the style of Browning's *Lost Leader*, he promises that if he hears Vauro haranguing in dubious company for some cause they have both championed, he will only ask him to continue "recounting stories packed with irony, for that is our job as clowns."[6]

The second half of the year was taken up largely, but not exclusively, with performances with three other young actors, based on Franca's, *Flight from the Senate*. Although both of them had been spent a great deal of time writing and publishing, the creative process was not complete until the printed word was transferred to the stage and when direct contact could be made with an audience. It was as if the book was a play-script *in fieri* which only completed its journey when transformed into a performance. Officially Dario's appearances were intended as a book launch, but while such events are normally sober affairs held in bookshops, Dario's preferred venues were theatres and the on-stage style was that of the comic or, as he now preferred to say, the clown. Readings from her book were interspersed with stand-up, improvised routines in which Dario extended his wife's acid portraits of politicians with satirical routines and barbs of his own.

Although the book was mainly concerned with Franca's time as senator, it also covered her campaigns against drugs, her anti-war activity and her involvement with groups which offered assistance to refugees. While the tour was still at the planning stage, there was an odd and unexpected hitch when the Vatican authorities revoked a booking Fo had made to appear in Rome at the Auditorium della Conciliazione, a theatre owned by the Church. Fo protested, pointing out that he and Franca had previously performed *Mistero buffo* in that venue and wondering how far down the reforms introduced by Pope Francis had percolated. The episode did him no harm, since it gave him wide publicity and several Roman theatres offered him their premises. He used the occasion to wonder aloud if he, a known admirer of the Pope, was being used by dark forces inside the Curia to obstruct Francis's reform agenda.

As he travelled around Italy, he gave his support to other causes in the places he visited. In January, he fetched up in Padua, where he called a press conference to express his concern over the precarious state of the Scrovegni Chapel, home of Giotto's masterpieces, but now in danger on account of the humidity levels. Years before, he had done a lecture-performance on Giotto, whose work he admired. Everyone agreed about the risks, but there was no consensus on what was to be done, leaving Dario worried that the immobility of the Council and its unwillingness to heed expert advice would lead to disaster. The vice-mayor, Ivo Rossi, turned up uninvited at the press conference to say that the matter was in hand. He asked Dario if he would like to plant a tree in a street dedicated to Nobel Prize winners, but unfortunately he had neglected to bring the tree.

In Bologna in February, he opened with a rewritten, revised version of his play on St Francis of Assisi, fifteen years after the first production, all proceeds going to the charity, *Terra Madre*, set up by Carlo Petrini, also founder in Italy of *Slow Food*, to help alleviate poverty in Africa. Dario's devotion to the two Francises, the pope and the saint, seemed to overlap, with life imitating art and art struggling to keep pace with life. His admiration for Pope Francis knew no bounds, so much so that he announced he had rewritten and restaged *Lu santo jullare Francesco* (The Holy Jester Francis) with the Pope in mind. Francis from Argentina seemed to Dario to embody all that he valued and admired in Francis of Assisi. Like the saint, he was in Dario's eyes a man of renewal, showing scant respect for established ways, demonstrating a bold willingness to stand up to the powerful, giving concrete expression to his love of the poor and his detestation of poverty, prepared to go any distance to secure peace and, whether dealing with politicians or cardinals in the curia, determined to avoid the easy way out, just like the saint. Dario reacted with annoyance to any attack on the Pope, so in June, having heard sly slights uttered against the Pope by certain Italian intellectuals, he even inserted a special scene in his defence into his performance in the Roman Arena in Verona. He underlined that he himself remained "an atheist, a Marxist-Leninist and a Darwinist," but he invited his Holiness to come and see a performance. Alas, the invitation was not taken up. However, on 22 June, RAI broadcast the play, the first work of his, as distinct from occasional appearances on individual shows, to be screened in seven years. The commonly accepted reason for this lapse of time was the dispute with the bishop of Assisi who had taken grave exception to Dario's doubts that all the works in the basilica were genuinely by Giotto. The church may reason in terms of eternity, but seven years were sufficient to implement a revolution in ecclesiastical attitudes.

There were other figures besides Grillo and the Pope who occupied Dario's mind. Matteo Renzi, previously Mayor of Florence, ousted Letta to become Prime Minister and leader of the Democratic Party. For many, not only on the left, Renzi was viewed as the last hope of Italy, the only politician with the strength to oppose Berlusconi, the only leader capable of bringing union to the fractious left and of introducing the reforms needed to enable the country to resolve the economic problems created by its chronic debt and the demands made by the EU. This was not Dario's assessment. Renzi's rise to power gave him no cause for hope, and he flayed him as mercilessly as he had done Giulio Andreotti, Amintore Fanfani and the other Christian Democrats in the 70s and 80s, or Berlusconi in the 90s. For Fo, Renzi, himself a Catholic, is no more than a new breed of Christian Democrat, but at the same time he represents the 21st century technocratic, pragmatic politician, bereft of vision, ideology or moral principle, as shown by his enthusiasm for measures to reduce the rights of employees who had lost their job, and his general indifference to the plight of working people who had borne the brunt of the austerity programme imposed after the great financial crash of 2008. Renzi's open door policy towards Berlusconi, and his willingness to work with him to introduce electoral reform, dismayed Dario. At times, he found it difficult to refer to him by name. "Deaths at work follow one after the other. The regime, exactly as it did yesterday, silences dissent. Look at the attitude of that Tuscan towards the working class. A horrible, piti-less, shameless attitude. He wants to cancel workers, sweep them away."[7] There was no need to identify the Tuscan.

New targets for his satire did not cause him to forget the older one. The news came that Berlusconi, who was known to have constructed a private mausoleum in the gardens of his villa near Milan, had had it extended and was even installing central heating. This titbit was too good an opportu-nity for Fo to miss. He wondered if Berlusconi, who was appearing in the dock in various courts in Italy, saw himself as a latter day Viking King. Fo fantasised, but it may have been more than a fantasy, that Berlusco-ni wished to be surrounded in death as in life by attendants, courtiers, servants, assorted flatterers and dancing girls performing bunga-bun-ga turns. Perhaps the place was being kept heated because Berlusconi thought he would only be hibernating until resuscitation.

Meantime, Dario himself was emerging in every sense on the side of the angels, or at least of the saints and their representatives on earth. In December 2014, his lecture-performance on St. Ambrose was final-ly broadcast on national television. It had been prepared as a TV pro-gramme in 2009, but had never made it to the screen. Dario and Franca gave seven sell-out performances at the time in the Piccolo, but the work did not reach the mass audience for which it had been intended. The date for the broadcast, 7 December, was deliberately, even provocatively, cho-sen to clash with the worldly, non-spiritual celebration of the feast of St Ambrose, patron saint of Milan, by an annual concert in La Scala to which all the great and good, or at least the fashionable and the powerful of the city, were invited. The official evening was rounded off with a sumptuous banquet to which only an inner élite was invited. Dario addressed anoth-er audience, telling the Milanese what manner of man their patron saint was, although his depiction of St Ambrose himself was not likely to please religious circles.

In his pronouncements on the environment and on society, and in spite of the hopes he places in Grillo, Dario sounded like a man puzzled and saddened by the turn events had taken. He feared, as he declared in tracts like *The Apocalypse Postponed*, that humankind's disregard for na-ture and his own habitat on earth would lead to a catastrophe if left un-checked. It seemed he found relief in his regard for the figure who oc-cupied the throne of St Peter, and behind him for St Francis. Ever the utopian optimist, or the anarchic dissident, he was most at home with political mischief makers, like Grillo, who threatened to overthrow the altars, pull down the pillars and cause the whole system to crash. Dario now preferred to advocate change of culture rather than purely political upheaval, so the gentle teaching of the Poor Man of Assisi was as useful as anything in Marx, Lenin or Darwin, his professed masters. Fo began to sound like a quasi-religious visionary without a properly defined creed.

In January 2015, he gave an interview to a Catholic newspaper, which after lambasting him in previous years for his blasphemy and disrespect for the clergy and the church was now one of his most devoted fans. The theme was Pope Francis, and the enlightened papal attitude on many topics of the day, notably his disgust with the war-like rhetoric of many statesmen, his sympathy for refugees, his opposition to the new racism which was becoming a force in several European countries, his attacks on the neo-liberal economy which the wealthy had constructed and the slave conditions in which many were condemned to live. Topics like the rights of working people and their dignity lost with unemployment had been forgotten by the left in Italy, but were remembered by the Pope. The ultimate model for Fo was once more St Francis of Assisi. "I who am a fanatic for St Francis. I have written four plays on him, I have carried out studies on him and have been close to the greatest European researchers on his life, have found in the Pope not only someone who says the same things as Francis but in the same language. He has understood that it is possible to say stupendous things while speaking with humility."[8]

In the same January, he wrote a more secular article which was vintage Fo in its use of a work from the classical tradition to satirise a modern scandal. The past ages that mattered to him now provided a mirror image for his own time, and there was little for his comfort in the spectacle. When confronted with a very modern scandal in Rome, Aristophanes provided a lens through which life could be examined, perhaps upside down. The spur to write the article was the interception by the Italian police of a phone call between a mafia boss, Massimo Carminati, and the head of a perfectly legal co-operative business, Salvatore Buzzi. The latter boasted of his ability to make money from the immigrant community. In his response, Fo feigned admiration for the culture of the mafia man who alluded to Tolkien and the territory known in his fiction as "middle earth." In all probability Carminati is more likely to have seen the film sequence than to have read the books, but he claims that he and his like inhabit middle earth and from that vantage point they control Rome. Dario pushes the fiction further back, to the creation of an imaginary country, Cloud-cuckoo-land, in Aristophanes' comedy *The Birds*. In Fo's summary, life in Athens had been made intolerable by the level of corruption and the contrast between the poverty of the many and the wealth of the few. Some decide to emigrate, but where to? Sicily is considered and rejected, but they hear of the mystic land beyond the clouds where the gods ensure that peace and harmony reign. Reaching that space requires the construction of wings which will allow humans to mix with the birds, but when they reach that space the birds turn out to be disillusioned with the gods who are every bit as depraved and self-seeking as the aristocracy in Greece. Dario is so enraptured of Greek theatre that he delights in retelling the plot and in explaining the wonders of ancient stage machinery which permitted the illusion of flight that he loses the original impulse to point the parallels between then and now. But perhaps it needed no underlining.[9]

REFERENCES

1   *Il Fatto Quotidiano*, 23 November 2014.

2   Private communication from Piero Sciotto, 30 January 2015.

3   *La Stampa, 10 December 2013*

4   Dario Fo and Giuseppina Manin *Un clown vi seppellirà*, Parma, Guanda, 2013.

5   *Il Fatto Quotidiano*, 2 June 2014.

6   *Il Fatto Quotidiano*, 7 December, 2013.

7   *Il Fatto Quotidiano*, cit.

8   *L'Avvenire*, 4 January 2015.

9   *Il Fatto Quotidiano*, 6 January 2015.

Chapter 8

THE EMERGING NOVELIST

In Luigi Pirandello's play *When You Are Somebody*, the unnamed, famous writer adopts a pseudonym and invents a new identity for himself to permit him to break with his past and give himself the licence to write in a new style. Dario had no recourse to any such stratagem, but at the age of 88 he was about to strike out in a new direction. In March 2014, he published what he viewed as his first novel, with Lucrezia Borgia as protagonist. The book was given the arresting title, *La figlia del Papa* (The Pope's Daughter), with copious illustrations by himself and a portrait on the cover of a young woman, taken to be Lucrezia, by Bartolomeo Veneto. The subject of the painting is at her most alluring, staring boldly at the viewer, hair over her shoulder, one breast tauntingly exposed.[1] The daughter in the title is indeed Lucrezia Borgia, the Pope is Alexander VI, the second of the Catalan dynasty to occupy that office, and the spur to writing was Dario's disgust with an international TV blockbuster, *The Borgias*, created by Neil Jordan and with a high profile cast including Jeremy Irons as Alexander VI, Holliday Grainger as Lucrezia, and Steven Berkoff and Derek Jacobi in minor roles. Dario considered the series in general and the depiction of Lucrezia in particular as up-market porn, and set himself on a course of reading and research to restore to her the dignity destroyed by the sensationalist treatment. Research was facilitated by the mass of books on the Borgia dynasty available in every language, including a history by Alexandre Dumas which Dario considered "stupendous." He also consulted the classic biography of Lucrezia by Ferdinand Gregorovius, and many others. However, his first reading was John Ford's Elizabethan tragedy, *'Tis pity She's a Whore*, although critics are divided on whether or not that work is inspired by Lucrezia's life.

If there is near unanimity in the assessment of the Borgia pope, Alexander VI, and his son, Machiavelli's hero and model prince, Cesare

Borgia, few characters have divided historical opinion as deeply as Lucrezia. For some, she was a woman devoid of all humanity and morality, a she-devil, evil incarnate, a murderer, a poisoner, a nymphomaniac psychopath who killed her lovers when they were no longer of any value or interest to her, a sexual predator guilty of incestuous love affairs. Dante Gabriel Rossetti has provided the classic depiction of her in this guise. In a portrait, he depicts her washing her hands to free herself of guilt after administering poison to her innocent husband, Duke Alfonso, while an image in a mirror behind her shows her father keeping Alfonso on his feet not out of humanity but to ensure that the poison permeates every part of his body. Lucrezia does not emerge much better from Donizetti's opera. There is an alternative view which sees her as a saintly, oppressed, wronged woman, maltreated, exploited, used and abused as a political pawn by male power at its most savage and satanic, that of her unscrupulous, deeply corrupt father and brother.

Dario was largely of the revisionist view. His reading convinced him that Lucrezia was a humane, courageous, highly cultured figure, misrepresented by historians. He formed the view that she was a great art lover, and an excellent, enlightened ruler of a city-state in an age when women were considered to be incapable of exercising power. The book he wrote takes the form of a historical novel, with footnotes referring to historical incident, dialogue freely invented and the author occasionally intervening in his own right. His first complaint with other works on Lucrezia, and on the Borgia family in general, was that she was viewed in isolation, out of the context of the Renaissance and the corrupt state of the church at the time, mention of which allowed him to make implicit comparisons with the reforming zeal of Pope Francis. Other revolutionary figures from the time, such as Copernicus, are introduced, although his discussions with the Pope do not concern the dispute over the geocentric or heliocentric universe, but the self-interested obstacles posed by the curia and cardinals to the reform of the church proposed by the Pope. Is this Alexander VI or Francis?

By the age of twelve, Lucrezia was aware of her parentage and found herself betrothed to the widowed Giovanni Sforza, Lord of Pesaro, a man more than twice her age and one whom she did not know and certainly could not love. When her husband had served his purpose, the marriage was dissolved by order of the Pope, and she was remarried to Alfonso, Prince of Salerno, whom in Dario's account she genuinely loved. The account of their relationship is written in a lyrical tone Dario rarely allows himself in his theatre. Alfonso was murdered in accordance with *raisons d'état*, irrespective of Lucrezia's feelings, when the Borgia alliances changed. She became governor of Spoleto, where she showed herself both an excellent civil ruler as well as an able military commander. For a brief time, she was de facto ruler of the church when her father was incapacitated. She was paired with a second Alfonso, ruler of Ferrara, one of the great centres of Renaissance poetry. Dario's purpose is to underline both her resistance to the powers that wished to treat a mere female as a pawn, and her drive to take control of her own destiny and to build on her native abilities. She was already an educated, cultured and perspicacious woman before her arrival at Ferrara, and she brought to the court there the greatest Humanist philosophers and writers. Here too she embarked on one of her many love affairs, with Pietro Bembo, himself one of the most distinguished poets and neo-platonic thinkers of the sixteenth century. The letters they exchanged are extant and Byron described them as "the prettiest love letters in the world."[2] She bore seven or eight children and died in childbirth.

The novel follows Lucrezia's life without the creation of suspense or the insertion of unexpected twists, but with vividly presented scenes. The balance between invention and fact in the historical novel has been long debated, and this novel is more history than fiction, although the author's viewpoint on the unfolding events, on the mores of the age and on the integrity of his heroine is always in evidence. Unsurprisingly the dialogue is bright and lively, which made the transfer to the stage straightforward. The premiere was held in the castle in Nepi which Lucrezia's father had refortified and refurbished for her when he was still a cardinal and then presented to her when he became Pope. Here she found refuge after her brother, Cesare Borgia, had the first Alfonso assassinated.

In September, the students at the Scuola d'Arte Drammatica Paolo Grassi put on *La Storia di Qu* (The Story of Qu), a work created by Dario in cooperation with them, inspired by stories of the Chinese writer, Lu Xun, set in the early days of Chinese revolution led by Mao. Dario made his entrance with a cage over his face on the sort which people in ancient China were compelled to wear if guilty of having offended the powers that be. His energies at that time were mainly devoted to a book-cum-performance on another woman, Maria Callas, intended from the outset for the stage. Given the title *Una Callas dimenticata* (A Forgotten Callas), it was written with Franca in the form of a playscript, entirely in dialogue, but it was unfinished at her death.[3] Dario continued on his own. He engaged a team of assistants, one typing the dialogue as he dictated and two young women artists working in an adjacent room on the canvases according to schemes sketched out by Dario, adding colour, improving perspective and suggesting decorative touches. He moved between the two places, asking for stronger colour here or there, and then returning to have the script he had just dictated read back to him. The delayed premiere and publication occurred at about the same time in late 2014. The final work is a biographical portrait, an act of homage to the great opera singer, following the stages of her life without any attempt to introduce extraneous elements of plot or action. Three actors read out the script, the first called simply and straightforwardly Dario, the second, the narrator, termed Actor, while the third, identified as Actress, is Maria Callas herself.

Dario had first met Maria Callas when he was in his twenties and an art student in the Brera in Milan. To earn pin money he and his friends worked as stage hands for La Scala helping to erect scenery. On one occasion as they were preparing the set, a young woman walked across the stage, stepping over the assorted pieces of debris scattered on the floor or hanging from the flies. Dario shouted a warning, but she replied she was there for a rehearsal. Work stopped as they all climbed down to hear Maria Callas rehearse Bellini's *Norma*. Later in life, she had a flat in Milan, and Dario got to know her better. Callas and Franca Rame shared the same dress designer.

The performance of *A Forgotten Callas* included excerpts from various operas, while some of Dario's images were projected onto a screen at the back of the stage. The final published version too carried these images, some as beguilingly erotic as those turned out in the last phase of his life by Picasso, on whom Dario had published a book in the previous year. One particularly striking canvas had in its original form shown Callas as Venus, completely naked, with tiny male figures clambering over her large limbs. In the book, she is shown in a recumbent pose, with one man seated on a breast, another dangling from her hair and others paddling around her on little boats. The reference now is not to the goddess but to *Gulliver's Travels* and in the script she reports on a dream in which she, who notoriously had problems with her weight, lies naked on a beach while her fellow actors and singers tuck into a sumptuous meal in a restaurant nearby. The beach is in Lilliput, and there she is surrounded by little men not ogling her but simply walking over and around her. "A pleasant dream," says the character Dario, to which the Actress retorts, "Pleasant but anguished, so much so that after the dream, I burst into desperate tears." Callas's body is depicted in several generous poses, some inspired by classical painting or ancient Greek sculpture, while others show her in more demure or elegant dress, often accompanied by the principal men in her life, Aristotle Onassis, Pippo de Stefano and Mario del Monaco. When she was alive, more than one music critic had commented on the exceptional dramatic qualities of Maria Callas, not just on stage as operatic actress but in the dramatic qualities of her voice itself, in her *bel canto* technique, in the variation of mood she successfully expressed with a vocal range which permitted her to move up and down scales, and in her deeply moving rendering of the coloratura passages of opera. Dario's dialogue is appreciative and admiring, not opera criticism under a new guise. He focuses on the drama and tragedies of Callas's life, not least on her battle with her body form, repeating the rumour or legend that to maintain her looks she, perhaps accidentally, swallowed a tapeworm which devoured the food she ate. Her temperamental behaviour is illustrated in several snappily told anecdotes and episodes. She suffered early humiliation when she found the doors of opera houses in America closed to her before her first success in Verona. Even when she had attained international fame, she endured further, extremely public, humiliation at the hands of Onassis, with whom she had a relationship over many years but who abruptly and callously abandoned her for Jacqueline Kennedy. Her last years were sad, as her voice lost its power perhaps for reasons linked to her dieting problems. She was only 54 when she died. Dario himself compared her fate to Medea, but if the tone of the piece is scarcely tragic, it avoids mawkish sentimentality.

He was no longer keen on long journeys by plane, but in November he was in Stuttgart for the opening of an exhibition of his work and a performance of *God Is Black*. There was one more book before 2014 was out, *Ciulla, il grande malfattore* (Ciulla, the Great Miscreant),[4] co-authored with Piero Sciotto. Piero is Sicilian and both he and Dario had long been fascinated by the figure of Paolo Ciulla, a native of Caltagirone, failed architect, aspiring artist, political agitator, anarchist, gentleman crook and forger of genius, even "the greatest forger in Italian history," who had just enough generosity towards the poor to make him, almost, a Robin Hood figure. He was also gay, which made life awkward in the nineteenth century, but he was a survivor and an opportunist. Writing the book together presented problems, as Piero has said: "Collaborating with Dario, in the sense of working together, is never an easy business. His presence is so strong and overwhelming that it makes life difficult for anyone who wants to establish an equal relationship. A vain hope! My main advantage was precisely the fact of having known both Dario and Franca so long."[5]

Sicilian history is dotted with such men, normally celebrated in song and legend in spite of, or perhaps because of, being bandits, but mainly for their prowess in besting the system. Ciulla was already the hero of a novel by Maria Attanasio, herself a native of Caltagirone.[6] The qualities that made him admired in Sicily are those which made him appeal to Dario and Piero, and the portrait is benevolent and largely uncritical. As they discussed the project, they were brought up short by connections revealed between Ciulla's biography and present-day conditions, as Piero explained: "leaving aside the mythical, legendary aspect of the story, in reconstructing the events we immediately had the sensation that we were working on a political script, as though we had discovered the DNA of modern Italy." This is the very nature of the historical novel as a genre, already apparent in Walter Scott and Alessandro Manzoni. Immersion in a period of history conceals under the skin a dialectic movement between the time of writing and the time portrayed. Perhaps the parallels are closer in Italy, but in any case the landmarks that came to the surface, as mentioned in the preface, are the depressingly familiar phenomena of "organised crime and corruption. The much flaunted innovations concern only the *techniques* of application. Nothing else. This story has been repeated in various forms for 150 years. It has not ended and who knows when it will end." Piero added: "We spoke about Italy today by desribing Italy yesterday, about *politics* without any direct reference to present-day politicians ... Everything the same? Nothing ever changing? In a certain sense, yes."

They decided not to work side by side, in part because Dario was always liable to be called away either by journalists or by assistants engaged on other work. They fixed on an acceptable division of labour. "Dario devoted himself to the reconstruction, imaginative at times, of the life of Paolo Ciulla. I attempted to document his life in a historical context. We both of us threw ourselves into the study of the history of Italy from Re-Unification to Fascism." Little is known about Ciulla's private life, but in the book he emerges as an anti-hero, almost at times as Dario's rogue twin. They shared the youthful desire to become artists, and Ciulla's talent as teller of tales is highlighted, although the comparison with Dario is in this case left unstated. More strongly, both displayed a tendency to view society as being awry, both possessed a wayward wit and displayed anarchic behaviour and disrespect for authority. As with *The Pope's Daughter*, the historical background, in this case post-Risorgimento Italy already home to banking scandals and political malfeasance, is carefully sketched out to explain the context within which Ciulla's life unfolds. That life was not lacking in colour and incident. After failing to make his way in Italy, he left for South America, where he was confined for years in a mental hospital in Brazil. During this period, he perfected his printing skills and put them to gainful use as a forger when he returned to Italy. He was discovered by the police by pure chance, and his trial became one of the *causes celebres* of *fin de siècle* Italy. Detailed legal records and journalistic accounts survive and they provide the bulk of the latter half of the book. Ciulla tested the judge's patience with his Puckish comments from the dock, but his irreverence won him a place in the pantheon of popular heroes.

Dario was now producing books as though from one of the mass production lines he had satirised in his first 'bourgeois' comedy, *Archangels Don't Play Pinball* (1959). In January 2015, another historical novel was published, set at the opposite end of Europe from Sicily, in eighteenth-century Denmark. *C'è un re pazzo in Danimarca* (There is a Mad King in Denmark) was authored by Dario alone, although Jacopo is credited with sparking his interest in the subject.[7] The characters and theme are those which provided the plot for the acclaimed Danish film, *A Royal Affair*, directed by Nikolai Arcel and released in 2012, although there is no reference to the film in the book. Both focus on the lives and policies of King Christian VII of Denmark and his son, Frederick, although Dario's novel covers a slightly longer time span.

Christian had intermittent periods of insanity and of lucidity, and in his clearer moments showed an awareness that there was something rotten in the state of Denmark. The ideas disseminated by the Enlightenment philosophers offered a way forward. It is not clear whether he reached this conclusion on his own or at the promptings of his English Queen, Caroline Matilda, and his private physician, the German Johann Friedrich Struensee, but both certainly encouraged him in his policies of innovation and reform. Struensee's admiration for the thought of Jean Jacques Rousseau was no secret. The king and the physician developed a deep friendship, which led to the king appointing Struensee Chief Minister of his government. Together they embarked on a far-reaching reform programme, including banning torture, releasing the peasants from burdens laid on them by their lords, introducing freedom of the press and ordering the liberation of slaves in the Danish empire. These policies outraged the conservative nobility, particularly the Queen Mother, Juliana Maria of Brunswick-Lüneburg, a figure who has all the ingrained malice, even more strongly portrayed in the film than in the book, of the wicked stepmother of fairy-tale. She was the second wife of Christian's father and had the additional motivation of wishing to see her son eventually succeed to the throne instead of Prince Frederick. A personal motif, the blossoming love of Struensee and Queen Caroline Matilda, complicates life in the palace even further and threatens to bring vengeful repercussions, although not from the king. One of the symptoms of Christian's psychological disturbance is that having fallen in love with his wife on their first meeting and having made her pregnant with Frederick, he loses interest in her. He views the growing intimacy between his wife and friend with equanimity, and is even happy to encourage Struensee to provide his wife with the affection he can no longer give her. This love affair is central to the plot of the film and provides some erotic scenes, but while it is recounted in Dario's novel, it does not have the same prominence. However, this novel is one of the few times in his career as writer that he attempts to endow his characters with an emotional life. He may have shown elsewhere a desire to enquire into eros and the erotic, but the interest was abstract and societal, not conveyed in the personal lives of his characters. In *There is a Mad King in Denmark,* there are moments where he describes with lyrical touches the joy of romantic union and physical contact between a loving couple, but this is not the leitmotif of the plot. This dimension is not his forte.

The queen becomes pregnant and has a daughter, who is believed to be Struensee's. In the film the two persuade the king to return to his wife's bed so that the child can be presented as his, but Dario makes no mention of this. The affair is revealed to the Queen Mother who has spies all over the palace, and it gives her and her allies the pretext to lead a counter-revolution and restore the *ancien régime.* Struensee is arrested, imprisoned, tortured and eventually beheaded, as is shown graphically in the film, but Dario shies away from any description of these events. His novel is mildly didactic in intent, as had been the story of Paolo Ciulla, and his interest is in society and reforming ideas. His involvement with eighteenth-century Denmark and the cult of reason and moderation that were part of the Enlightenment is deep and genuine, but it is never hard to glimpse contemporary Italy behind the Danish façade.

Caroline Matilda is separated from her children and sent into exile. The film ends on that note, except for one appendix scene when the children, now adults, are shown reading a letter she had written to them about what had taken place, and are spurred to reintroduce all the rescinded reforms. The fall of Struensee, however, takes place half way through the novel. The narrative and the authorial voice of this first part have greater assurance than in *The Pope's Daughter*, and neither is there any sign of the overt, sometimes intrusive or heavy irony of the sort employed elsewhere. This is a more soberly written work, produced by an author who recounts the eighteenth century, its culture and behaviour with a lightness of touch which carries echoes of Italo Calvino. Irony in this case springs from the tone of disbelief and incredulity which is intrinsic to the narrative itself and which seems demanded by a sane response to the unfolding events. Nor are the illustrations to the novel the exuberant, riotous sketches which had embellished other works in this period, but restrained, highly professional full-length or head-and-shoulders portraits of the chief players, framed and finished in the style visible on the walls of eighteenth-century mansions all over Europe. They resemble the work of a master forger.

The novel changes tack in the second half to follow the young prince Frederick as he grows up and is, in spite of difficulties, able to meet with his father and his sister. All three are under surveillance and lodged in separate apartments of the royal palace, but with the help of one of the guards they manage to arrange to see each other. The central focus of the narrative becomes the spread of discontent in the country and the diffusion of Enlightenment philosophy, all this in Denmark decades before the Fall of the Bastille. The people are stirring, the need for rejection of feudal ways is making itself felt, but change will be top down, with the ascent of Frederick to the position of Regent. This novel is no allegory but glances at modern Italy are strong, especially in the account of the dispute in the Council called to install Frederick in office. One of the causes of the ensuing riot by the nobles was the Prince's insistence that tax evasion must be ended. The grandees of modern Italy protested against similar measure with equal vehemence. The new society decreed by Prince Frederick, with the introduction of universal education, wide reaching agricultural reform in the interests of the peasant class and the insistence on reasoned argument and debate makes Denmark seem like the yearned for Utopia. Dario concludes the novel in his own voice, repeating the fable he had recounted at Franca's funeral, of Adam and Eve being offered the choice between two trees and rejecting the one which promised immortality in favour of the one which gave the prospect of love and knowledge.

Only a mad king could dream of a Utopia for all his subjects, or citizens, not just for the oligarchy ... but then in history, as Dario notes in bitter words on Horatio Nelson and the Battle of Copenhagen, there was war between Britain and France, with Denmark ending up on the losing side.

There is more to come from Dario Fo. All passion is not spent, all outrage is not quietened. He has a place as the clown prince or jester, never the licensed court fool but the buffoon figure who in medieval England could also be known as the truth-teller. A biography of a living person who is still active can never end with a neat conclusion. Dario gives every impression of being at peace with himself, even if he is now deprived of the company of, as he repeats, the only woman he loved. In a newspaper piece, he complained to his interviewer that he had endured much abuse when he was younger, from his own profession as well as in the political domain. "Actors denied I was an author and authors did the same. You are nothing more than an actor dressed up as an author," he said he was told, but he was able to add, "I remained outside every category and I managed very well. I have had a stupendous life."[8] Now on the cusp of his ninetieth birthday, whatever slings and arrows have been aimed at him in public, is this a statement of as full a success in the pursuit of happiness as is granted to a human being?

REFERENCES

1   Dario Fo, *La figlia del Papa*, Milan, Chiarelettere, 2014.
2   Lucrezia Borgia & Pietro Bembo, translated by Hugh Shankland, *The Prettiest Love Letters in the World*, London, Collins Harvill, 1987.
3   Dario Fo e Franca Rame, *Una Callas dimenticata*, Moden, Franco Cosimo Panini, 2014.
4   Dario Fo and Piero Sciotto, *Ciulla, il grande malfattore*, Parma, Guanda, 2014.
5   Personal communication from Piero Sciotto.
6   Maria Attanasio, *Il falsario di Caltagirone*, Palermo, Sellerio, 2007: cf also, Pietro Nicolosi, *Paolo Ciulla, il falsario*, Catania, Tringale, 1984. Both books were consulted by Fo and Sciotto.
7   Dario Fo, *C'è un re pazzo in Danimarca*, Milan, Chiarelettere, 2015.
8   *Il Fatto Quotidiano*, 23 November 2014.

1999 - ORIGINAL DARIO FO DRAWINGS FOR "TAROCCHI" PUB-
LISHED BY CASA EDITRICE DAL NEGRO.

1999 - Original Dario Fo Drawings for "Tarocchi" Published by Casa Editrice Dal Negro.

Within the drawing:

DEDICATO
ALLE DONNE
SCHIAVE
DELL'
AFGANISTAN

Dario Fo
2001

2001 - DARIO FO DRAWING DEDICATED TO AFGHAN WOMEN.

PUBBLICITÁ TELEVISIVA

2001 - Dario Fo drawing, in cooperation with Matteo De Martino, used in the script of "Il grande bugiardo, (The Great Liar), a satirical monologue on Silvio Berlusconi, performed at the "Palalido di Milano," 10 May 2001, during rally in support of "Miracolo a Milano," a political movement with Franca Rame as head of list of candidates at Municipal elections

2002 - POSTER FOR "DA TANGENTOPOLI ALL''IRRESISTIBILE ASCE-
SA DI UBU BAS" (FROM BRIBESVILLE TO THE UNSTOPPABLE RISE
OF UBU BAS), BY AND WITH FRANCA RAME AND DARIO FO AT
TEATRO SMERALDO, MILAN.

2004 - Painting by Dario Fo in cooperation with Matteo De Martino for Performance-Lecture "Caravaggio al Tempo di Caravaggio" (Caravaggio in His Own Time), broadcast on Rai3

2006 - MATERIAL DRAWN BY DARIO FO IN HIS (UNSUCCESSFUL)
CAMPAIGN FOR ELECTION AS MAYOR OF MILAN

2006 - MATERIAL DRAWN BY DARIO FO IN HIS (UNSUCCESSFUL) CAMPAIGN FOR ELECTION AS MAYOR OF MILAN

2006 - Franca Rame at lunch with President of the Senate
and other senators

2006 - DARIO FO PAINTING, AFTER HIERONYMOUS BOSCH

2006 - DARIO FO PAINTING, AFTER HIERONYMOUS BOSCH

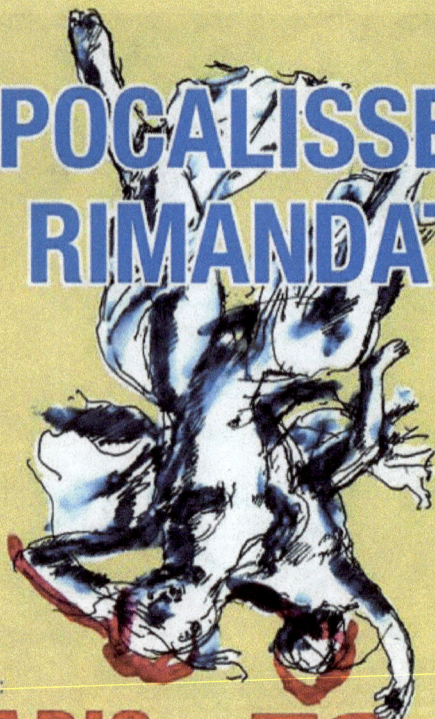

L'APOCALISSE RIMANDATA

CTFR presenta:

DARIO JACOPO FO & FRANCA RAME

2008 - THE FO-RAME THEATRE COMPANY PRESENTS "L'APOCALISSE RIMANDATA" (THE APOCALYPSE POSTPONED) WITH FRANCA RAME, DARIO AND JACOPO FO

2008 - PAINTING BY DARIO FO FOR CAMPAIGN BY RITA BORSELLI-
NO FOR ELECTION AS PRESIDENT OF THE SICILIAN REGION

2010 - ILLUSTRATION BY DARIO FO FOR "L'OSCENO E' SACRO"
(THE OBSCENE IS SACRED), BY DARIO FO AND FRANCA RAME,
PUBLISHED BY CASA EDITRICE GUANDA.

2010 - Illustration by Dario Fo for "L'osceno e' sacro" (The Obscene is Sacred), by Dario Fo and Franca Rame, published by Casa Editrice Guanda.

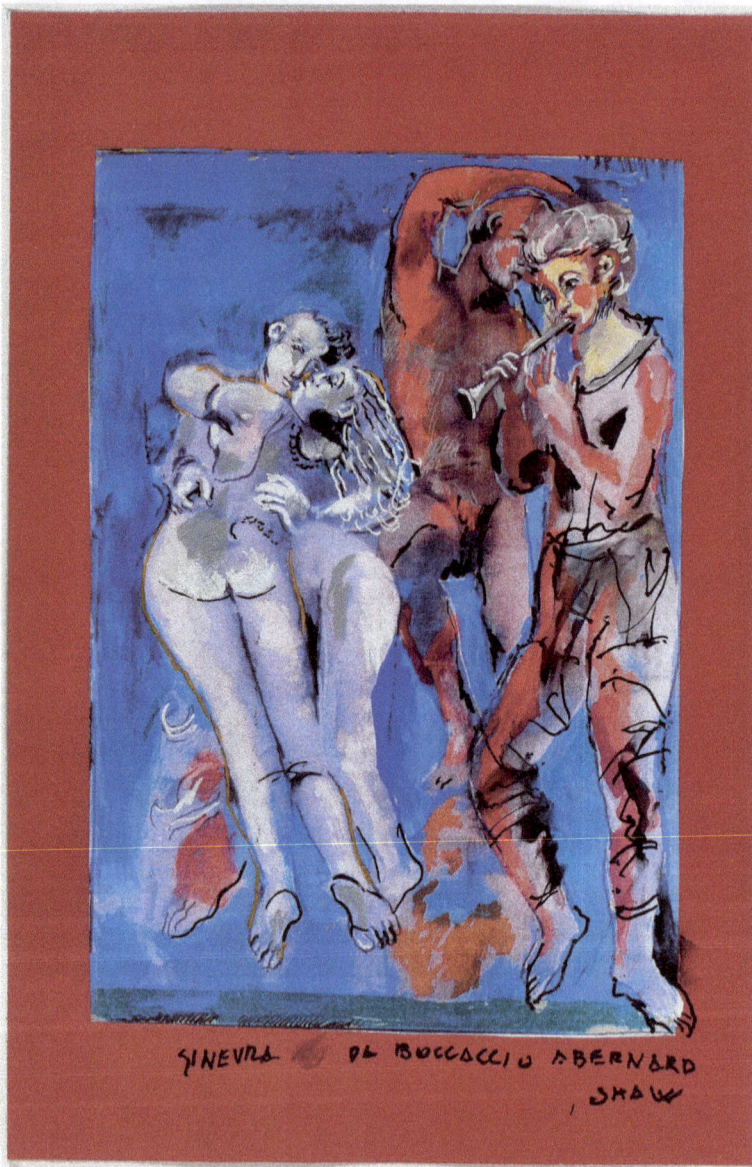

2010 - Painting by Dario Fo for Exhibition: inspired by Boccaccio's Decameron

www.ingramcontent.com/pod-product-compliance
Lightning Source LLC
Chambersburg PA
CBHW062111080426
42734CB00012B/2825